THE
KYBALION

&

THE
EMERALD TABLET
OF HERMES

British Library Cataloguing in Publication Data

A catalogue record for this book is available from the British Library

ISBN-13: 978-1-911405-26-9

Cover Illustration:
The Emerald Tablet of Hermes
(Modern Reconstruction)

Title Page:
Hermes Trismegistus.
Woodcut. De Chemica Senioris (1566)

TO HERMES TRISMEGISTUS
KNOWN BY THE ANCIENT EGYPTIANS AS
"THE GREAT GREAT"
AND
"MASTER OF MASTERS"
THIS LITTLE VOLUME
OF HERMETIC TEACHING
IS REVERENTLY DEDICATED

THE KYBALION

Contents

THE EMERALD TABLET OF HERMES

Contents

THE KYBALION

A Study of
The Hermetic Philosophy of
Ancient Egypt and Greece

BY THREE INITIATES

"THE LIPS OF WISDOM ARE CLOSED,
EXCEPT TO THE EARS OF UNDERSTANDING"

INTRODUCTION

We take great pleasure in presenting to the attention of students and investigators of the Secret Doctrines this little work based upon the world-old Hermetic Teachings. There has been so little written upon this subject, not withstanding the countless references to the Teachings in the many works upon occultism, that the many earnest searchers after the Arcane Truths will doubtless welcome the appearance of this present volume.

The purpose of this work is not the enunciation of any special philosophy or doctrine, but rather is to give to the students a statement of the Truth that will serve to reconcile the many bits of occult knowledge that they may have acquired, but which are apparently opposed to each other and which often serve to discourage and disgust the beginner in the study. Our intent is not to erect a new Temple of Knowledge, but rather to place in the hands of the student a Master-Key with which he may open the many inner doors in the Temple of Mystery through the main portals he has already entered.

There is no portion of the occult teachings possessed by the world which have been so closely guarded as the fragments of the Hermetic Teachings which have come down to us over the tens of centuries which have elapsed since the lifetime of its great founder, Hermes Trismegistus, the "scribe of the gods," who dwelt in old Egypt in the days when the present race of men was in its infancy. Contemporary with Abraham, and, if the legends be true, an instructor of that venerable sage, Hermes was, and is, the Great Central Sun of Occultism, whose rays have served to illumine the countless teachings which have been promulgated since his time. All the fundamental and basic teachings embedded in the esoteric teachings of every race may be traced back to Hermes. Even the most ancient teachings of India undoubtedly have their roots in the original Hermetic Teachings.

From the land of the Ganges many advanced occultists wandered to the land of Egypt, and sat at the feet of the Master. From him they obtained the Master-Key which explained and reconciled their divergent views, and thus the Secret Doctrine was firmly established. From other lands also came the learned ones, all of whom regarded Hermes as the Master of Masters, and his influence was so great that in spite of the many wanderings from the path on the part of the centuries of teachers in these different lands, there may still be found a certain basic resemblance and correspondence which underlies the many and often quite divergent theories entertained and taught by the occultists of these different lands today. The student of Comparative Religions will be able to perceive the influence of the Hermetic Teachings in every religion worthy of the name, now known to man, whether it be a dead religion or one in full vigor in our own times. There is always certain correspondence in spite of the contradictory features, and the Hermetic Teachings act as the Great Reconciler.

The lifework of Hermes seems to have been in the direction of planting the great Seed-Truth which has grown and blossomed in so many strange forms, rather than to establish a school of philosophy which would dominate, the world's thought. But, nevertheless, the original truths taught by him have been kept intact in their original purity by a few men each age, who, refusing great numbers of half-developed students and followers, followed the Hermetic custom and reserved their truth for the few who were ready to comprehend and master it. From lip to ear the truth has been handed down among the few. There have always been a few Initiates in each generation, in the various lands of the earth, who kept alive the sacred flame of the Hermetic Teachings, and such have always been willing to use their lamps to re-light the lesser lamps of the outside world, when the light of truth grew dim, and clouded by reason of neglect, and when the wicks became clogged with foreign matter. There were always a few to tend faithfully the altar of the Truth, upon which was kept alight the Perpetual Lamp of Wisdom. These men devoted their lives to the labor of love which the poet has so well stated in his lines:

"O, let not the flame die out! Cherished age after age in its dark cavern – in its holy temples cherished. Fed by pure ministers of love – let not the flame die out!"

These men have never sought popular approval, nor numbers of followers. They are indifferent to these things, for they know how few there are in each generation who are ready for the truth, or who would recognize it if it were presented to them. They reserve the "strong meat for men," while others furnish the "milk for babes." They reserve their pearls of wisdom for the few elect, who recognize their value and who wear them in their crowns, instead of casting them before the materialistic vulgar swine, who would trample them in the mud and mix them with their disgusting mental food. But still these men have never forgotten or overlooked the original teachings of Hermes, regarding the passing on of the words of truth to those ready to receive it, which teaching is stated in The Kybalion as follows: "Where fall the footsteps of the Master, the ears of those ready for his Teaching open wide." And again: "When the ears of the student are ready to hear, then cometh the lips to fill them with wisdom." But their customary attitude has always been strictly in accordance with the other Hermetic aphorism, also in The Kybalion: "The lips of Wisdom are closed, except to the ears of Understanding."

There are those who have criticized this attitude of the Hermetists, and who have claimed that they did not manifest the proper spirit in their policy of seclusion and reticence. But a moment's glance back over the pages of history will show the wisdom of the Masters, who knew the folly of attempting to teach to the world that which it was neither ready or willing to receive. The Hermetists have never sought to be martyrs, and have, instead, sat silently aside with a pitying smile on their closed lips, while the "heathen raged noisily about them" in their customary amusement of putting to death and torture the honest but misguided enthusiasts who imagined that they could force upon a race of barbarians the truth capable of being understood only by the elect who had advanced along The Path.

And the spirit of persecution has not as yet died out in the land. There are certain Hermetic Teachings, which, if publicly promulgated, would bring down upon the teachers a great cry of scorn and revilement from the multitude, who would again raise the cry of "Crucify! Crucify."

In this little work we have endeavored to give you an idea of the fundamental teachings of The Kybalion, striving to give you the working Principles, leaving you to apply them yourselves, rather than attempting to work out the teaching in detail. If you are a true student, you will be able to work out and apply these Principles – if not, then you must develop yourself into one, for otherwise the Hermetic Teachings will be as "words, words, words" to you.

THE THREE INITIATES

CHAPTER I

THE HERMETIC PHILOSOPHY

"The lips of wisdom are closed, except to the ears of Understanding"

The Kybalion.

From old Egypt have come the fundamental esoteric and occult teachings which have so strongly influenced the philosophies of all races, nations and peoples, for several thousand years. Egypt, the home of the Pyramids and the Sphinx, was the birthplace of the Hidden Wisdom and Mystic Teachings. From her Secret Doctrine all nations have borrowed. India, Persia, Chaldea, Medea, China, Japan, Assyria, ancient Greece and Rome, and other ancient countries partook liberally at the feast of knowledge which the Hierophants and Masters of the Land of Isis so freely provided for those who came prepared to partake of the great store of Mystic and Occult Lore which the masterminds of that ancient land had gathered together.

In ancient Egypt dwelt the great Adepts and Masters who have never been surpassed, and who seldom have been equaled, during the centuries that have taken their processional flight since the days of the Great Hermes. In Egypt was located the Great Lodge of Lodges of the Mystics. At the doors of her Temples entered the Neophytes who afterward, as Hierophants, Adepts, and Masters, traveled to the four corners of the earth, carrying with them the precious knowledge which they were ready, anxious, and willing to pass on to those who were ready to receive the same. All students of the Occult recognize the debt that they owe to these venerable Masters of that ancient land.

But among these great Masters of Ancient Egypt there once dwelt one of whom Masters hailed as "The Master of Masters." This man, if "man" indeed he was, dwelt in Egypt in the earliest days. He was known as Hermes Trismegistus. He was the father of the Occult Wisdom; the founder of Astrology; the discoverer of Alchemy. The details of his life story are lost to history, owing to the lapse of the years, though several of the ancient countries disputed with each other in their claims to the honor of having furnished his birthplace – and this thousands of years ago. The date of his sojourn in Egypt, in that his last incarnation on this planet, is not now known, but it has been fixed at the early days of the oldest dynasties of Egypt – long before the days of Moses. The best authorities regard him as a contemporary of Abraham, and some of the Jewish traditions go so far as to claim that Abraham acquired a portion of his mystic knowledge from Hermes himself.

As the years rolled by after his passing from this plane of life (tradition recording that he lived three hundred years in the flesh), the Egyptians deified Hermes, and made him one of their gods, under the name of Thoth. Years after, the people of Ancient Greece also made him one of their many gods – calling him "Hermes, the god of Wisdom." The Egyptians revered his memory for many centuries – yes, tens of centuries – calling him "the Scribe of the Gods," and bestowing upon him, distinctively, his ancient title, "Trismegistus," which means "the thrice-great"; "the great-great"; "the greatest-great"; etc. In all the ancient lands, the name of Hermes Trismegistus was revered, the name being synonymous with the "Fount of Wisdom."

Even to this day, we use the term "hermetic" in the sense of "secret"; "sealed so that nothing can escape"; etc., and this by reason of the fact that the followers of Hermes always observed the principle of secrecy in their teachings. They did not believe in "casting pearls before swine," but rather held to the teaching "milk for babes"; "meat for strong men," both of which maxims are familiar to readers of the Christian scriptures, but both of which had been used by the Egyptians for centuries before the Christian era.

And this policy of careful dissemination of the truth has always characterized the Hermetics, even unto the present day. The Hermetic Teachings are to be found in all lands, among all religions, but never identified with any particular country, nor with any particular religious sect. This because of the warning of the ancient teachers against allowing the Secret Doctrine to become crystallized into a creed. The wisdom of this caution is apparent to all students of history. The ancient occultism of India and Persia degenerated, and was largely lost, owing to the fact that the teachers became priests, and so mixed theology with the philosophy, the result being that the occultism of India and Persia has been gradually lost amidst the mass of religious superstition, cults, creeds and "gods." So it was with Ancient Greece and Rome. So it was with the Hermetic Teachings of the Gnostics and Early Christians, which were lost at the time of Constantine, whose iron hand smothered philosophy with the blanket of theology, losing to the Christian Church that which was its very essence and spirit, and causing it to grope throughout several centuries before it found the way back to its ancient faith, the indications apparent to all careful observers in this Twentieth Century being that the Church is now struggling to get back to its ancient mystic teachings.

But there were always a few faithful souls who kept alive the Flame, tending it carefully, and not allowing its light to become extinguished. And thanks to these staunch hearts, and fearless minds, we have the truth still with us. But it is not found in books, to any great extent. It has been passed along from Master to Student; from Initiate to Hierophant; from lip to ear. When it was written down at all, its meaning was veiled in terms of alchemy and astrology so that only those possessing the key could read it aright. This was made necessary in order to avoid the persecutions of the theologians of the Middle Ages, who fought the Secret Doctrine with fire and sword; stake, gibbet and cross. Even to this day there will be found but few reliable books on the Hermetic Philosophy, although there are countless references to it in many books written on various phases of Occultism. And yet, the Hermetic Philosophy is the only Master Key which will open all the doors of the Occult Teachings!

In the early days, there was a compilation of certain Basic Hermetic Doctrines, passed on from teacher to student, which was known as "THE KYBALION," the exact significance and meaning of the term having been lost for several centuries. This teaching, however, is known to many to whom it has descended, from mouth to ear, on throughout the centuries. Its precepts have never been written down, or printed, so far as we know. It was merely a collection of maxims, axioms, and precepts, which were non-understandable to outsiders, but which were readily understood by students, after the axioms, maxims, and precepts had been explained and exemplified by the Hermetic Initiates to their Neophytes. These teachings really constituted the basic principles of "The Art of Hermetic Alchemy," which, contrary to the general belief, dealt in the mastery of Mental Forces, rather than Material Elements – the Transmutation of one kind of Mental Vibrations into others, instead of the changing of one kind of metal into another. The legends of the "Philosopher's Stone" which would turn base metal into Gold, was an allegory relating to Hermetic Philosophy, readily understood by all students of true Hermeticism.

In this little book, of which this is the First Lesson, we invite our students to examine into the Hermetic Teachings, as set forth in THE KYBALION, and as explained by ourselves, humble students of the Teachings, who, while bearing the title of Initiates, are still students at the feet of HERMES, the Master. We herein give you many of the maxims, axioms and precepts of THE KYBALION, accompanied by explanations and illustrations which we deem likely to render the teachings more easily comprehended by the modern student, particularly as the original text is purposely veiled in obscure terms.

The original maxims, axioms, and precepts of THE KYBALION are printed herein, in italics, the proper credit being given. Our own work is printed in the regular way, in the body of the work. We trust that the many students to whom we now offer this little work will derive as much benefit from the study of its pages as have the many who have gone on before, treading the same Path to Mastery throughout the centuries that have passed since the times of HERMES TRISMEGISTUS – the Master of Masters – the Great-Great. In the words of THE KYBALION:

Where fall the footsteps of the Master, the ears of those
ready for his Teaching open wide. – The Kybalion.

When the ears of the student are ready to hear, then cometh the lips to fill them with Wisdom. – The Kybalion.

So that according to the Teachings, the passage of this book to those ready for the instruction will attract the attention of such as are prepared to receive the Teaching. And, likewise, when the pupil is ready to receive the truth, then will this little book come to him, or her. Such is The Law. The Hermetic Principle of Cause and Effect, in its aspect of The Law of Attraction, will bring lips and ear together – pupil and book in company. So mote it be!

CHAPTER II

THE SEVEN HERMETIC PRINCIPLES

"The Principles of Truth are Seven; he who knows these, understandingly, possesses the Magic Key before whose touch all the Doors of the Temple fly open." – The Kybalion.

The Seven Hermetic Principles, upon which the entire Hermetic Philosophy is based, are as follows:

1. The Principle of Mentalism.
2. The Principle of Correspondence.
3. The Principle of Vibration.
4. The Principle of Polarity.
5. The Principle of Rhythm.
6. The Principle of Cause and Effect.
7. The Principle of Gender.

These Seven Principles will be discussed and explained as we proceed with these lessons. A short explanation of each, however, may as well be given at this point.

1. The Principle of Mentalism

"THE ALL IS MIND; The Universe is Mental." – The Kybalion.

This Principle embodies the truth that "All is Mind." It explains that THE ALL (which is the Substantial Reality underlying all the outward manifestations and appearances which we know under the terms of "The Material Universe"; the "Phenomena of Life"; "Matter"; "Energy"; and, in short, all that is apparent to our material senses) is SPIRIT which in itself is UNKNOWABLE and UNDEFINABLE, but which may be considered and thought of as AN UNIVERSAL, INFINITE, LIVING MIND. It also explains that all the phenomenal world or universe is simply a Mental Creation of THE ALL, subject to the Laws of Created Things, and that the universe, as a whole, and in its parts or units, has its existence in the Mind of THE ALL, in which Mind we "live and move and have our being." This Principle, by establishing the Mental Nature of the Universe, easily explains all of the varied mental and psychic phenomena that occupy such a large portion of the public attention, and which, without such explanation, are non-understandable and defy scientific treatment. An understanding of this great

Hermetic Principle of Mentalism enables the individual to readily grasp the laws of the Mental Universe, and to apply the same to his well-being and advancement. The Hermetic Student is enabled to apply intelligently the great Mental Laws, instead of using them in a haphazard manner. With the Master-Key in his possession, the student may unlock the many doors of the mental and psychic temple of knowledge, and enter the same freely and intelligently. This Principle explains the true nature of "Energy," "Power," and "Matter," and why and how all these are subordinate to the Mastery of Mind. One of the old Hermetic Masters wrote, long ages ago: "He who grasps the truth of the Mental Nature of the Universe is well advanced on The Path to Mastery." And these words are as true today as at the time they were first written. Without this Master-Key, Mastery is impossible, and the student knocks in vain at the many doors of The Temple.

2. The Principle of Correspondence

"As above, so below; as below, so above." – The Kybalion.

This Principle embodies the truth that there is always a Correspondence between the laws and phenomena of the various planes of Being and Life. The old Hermetic axiom ran in these words: "As above, so below; as below, so above." And the grasping of this Principle gives one the means of solving many a dark paradox, and hidden secret of Nature. There are planes beyond our knowing, but when we apply the Principle of Correspondence to them we are able to understand much that would otherwise be unknowable to us. This Principle is of universal application and manifestation, on the various planes of the material, mental, and spiritual universe – it is an Universal Law. The ancient Hermetists considered this Principle as one of the most important mental instruments by which man was able to pry aside the obstacles which hid from view the Unknown. Its use even tore aside the Veil of Isis to the extent that a glimpse of the face of the goddess might be caught. Just as a knowledge of the Principles of Geometry enables man to measure distant suns and their movements, while seated in his observatory, so a knowledge of the Principle of Correspondence enables Man to reason intelligently from the Known to the Unknown. Studying the monad, he understands the archangel.

3. The Principle of Vibration

"Nothing rests; everything moves; everything vibrates."
– The Kybalion.

This Principle embodies the truth that "everything is in motion"; "everything vibrates"; "nothing is at rest"; facts which Modern Science endorses, and which each new scientific discovery tends to verify. And yet this Hermetic Principle was enunciated thousands of years ago, by the Masters of Ancient Egypt. This Principle explains that the differences between different manifestations of Matter, Energy, Mind, and even Spirit, result largely from varying rates of Vibration. From THE ALL, which is Pure Spirit, down to the grossest form of Matter, all is in vibration – the higher the vibration, the higher the position in the scale. The vibration of Spirit is at such an infinite rate of intensity and rapidity that it is practically at rest – just as a rapidly moving wheel seems to be motionless. And at the other end of the scale, there are gross forms of matter whose vibrations are so low as to seem at rest. Between these poles, there are millions upon millions of varying degrees of vibration. From corpuscle and electron, atom and molecule, to worlds and universes, everything is in vibratory motion. This is also true on the planes of energy and force (which are but varying degrees of vibration); and also on the mental planes (whose states depend upon vibrations); and even on to the spiritual planes. An understanding of this Principle, with the appropriate formulas, enables Hermetic students to control their own mental vibrations as well as those of others. The Masters also apply this Principle to the conquering of Natural phenomena, in various ways. "He who understands the Principle of Vibration, has grasped the scepter of power," says one of the old writers.

4. The Principle of Polarity

"Everything is Dual; everything has poles; everything has its pair of opposites; like and unlike are the same; opposites are identical in nature, but different in degree; extremes meet; all truths are but half-truths; all paradoxes may be reconciled." – The Kybalion.

This Principle embodies the truth that "everything is dual"; "everything has two poles"; "everything has its pair of opposites," all of which were old Hermetic axioms. It explains the old paradoxes, that have perplexed so many, which have been stated as follows: "Thesis and antithesis are identical in nature, but different in degree"; "opposites are the same, differing only in degree"; "the pairs of opposites may be reconciled"; "extremes meet"; "everything is and isn't, at the same time"; "all truths are but half-truths"; "every truth is half-false"; "there are two sides to everything," etc., etc., etc. It explains that in everything there are two poles, or opposite aspects, and that "opposites" are really only the two extremes of the same thing, with many varying degrees between them. To illustrate: Heat and Cold, although "opposites," are really the same thing, the differences consisting merely of degrees of the same thing. Look at your thermometer and see if you can discover where "heat" terminates and "cold" begins! There is no such thing as "absolute heat" or "absolute cold" –

the two terms "heat" and "cold" simply indicate varying degrees of the same thing, and that "same thing" which manifests as "heat" and "cold" is merely a form, variety, and rate of Vibration. So "heat" and "cold" are simply the "two poles" of that which we call "Heat" – and the phenomena attendant thereupon are manifestations of the Principle of Polarity. The same Principle manifests in the case of "Light and Darkness," which are the same thing, the difference consisting of varying degrees between the two poles of the phenomena. Where does "darkness" leave off, and "light" begin? What is the difference between "Large and Small"? Between "Hard and Soft"? Between "Black and White"? Between "Sharp and Dull"? Between "Noise and Quiet"? Between "High and Low"? Between "Positive and Negative"? The Principle of Polarity explains these paradoxes, and no other Principle can supersede it. The same Principle operates on the Mental Plane. Let us take a radical and extreme example – that of "Love and Hate," two mental states apparently totally different. And yet there are degrees of Hate and degrees of Love, and a middle point in which we use the terms "Like or Dislike," which shade into each other so gradually that sometimes we are at a loss to know whether we "like" or "dislike" or "neither." And all are simply degrees of the same thing, as you will see if you will but think a moment. And, more than this (and considered of more importance by the Hermetists), it is possible to change the vibrations of Hate to the vibrations of Love, in one's own mind, and in the minds of others. Many of you, who read these lines, have had personal experiences of the involuntary rapid transition from Love to Hate, and the reverse, in your own case and that of others. And you will therefore realize the possibility of this being accomplished by the use of the Will, by means of the Hermetic formulas. "Good and Evil" are but the poles of the same thing, and the Hermetist understands the art of transmuting Evil into Good, by means of an application of the Principle of Polarity. In short, the "Art of Polarization" becomes a phase of "Mental Alchemy" known and practiced by the ancient and modern Hermetic Masters. An understanding of the Principle will enable one to change his own Polarity, as well as that of others, if he will devote the time and study necessary to master the art.

5. The Principle of Rhythm

"Everything flows, out and in; everything has its tides; all things rise and fall; the pendulum-swing manifests in everything; the measure of the swing to the right is the measure of the swing to the left; rhythm compensates."

– The Kybalion.

This Principle embodies the truth that in everything there is manifested a measured motion, to and fro; a flow and inflow; a swing backward and forward; a pendulum-like movement; a tide-like ebb and flow; a high-tide and low-tide;

18

between the two poles which exist in accordance with the Principle of Polarity described a moment ago. There is always an action and a reaction; an advance and a retreat; a rising and a sinking. This is in the affairs of the Universe, suns, worlds, men, animals, mind, energy, and matter. This law is manifest in the creation and destruction of worlds; in the rise and fall of nations; in the life of all things; and finally in the mental states of Man (and it is with this latter that the Hermetists find the understanding of the Principle most important). The Hermetists have grasped this Principle, finding its universal application, and have also discovered certain means to overcome its effects in themselves by the use of the appropriate formulas and methods. They apply the Mental Law of Neutralization. They cannot annul the Principle, or cause it to cease its operation, but they have learned how to escape its effects upon themselves to a certain degree depending upon the Mastery of the Principle. They have learned how to USE it, instead of being USED BY it. In this and similar methods, consist the Art of the Hermetists. The Master of Hermetics polarizes himself at the point at which he desires to rest, and then neutralizes the Rhythmic swing of the pendulum which would tend to carry him to the other pole. All individuals who have attained any degree of Self-Mastery do this to a certain degree, more or less unconsciously, but the Master does this consciously, and by the use of his Will, and attains a degree of Poise and Mental Firmness almost impossible of belief on the part of the masses who are swung backward and forward like a pendulum. This Principle and that of Polarity have been closely studied by the Hermetists, and the methods of counteracting, neutralizing, and USING them form an important part of the Hermetic Mental Alchemy.

6. The Principle of Cause and Effect

"Every Cause has its Effect; every Effect has its Cause; everything happens according to Law; Chance is but a name for Law not recognized; there are many planes of causation, but nothing escapes the Law." – The Kybalion.

This Principle embodies the fact that there is a Cause for every Effect; an Effect from every Cause. It explains that: "Everything Happens according to Law"; that nothing ever "merely happens"; that there is no such thing as Chance; that while there are various planes of Cause and Effect, the higher dominating the lower planes, still nothing ever entirely escapes the Law. The Hermetists understand the art and methods of rising above the ordinary plane of Cause and Effect, to a certain degree, and by mentally rising to a higher plane they become Causers instead of Effects. The masses of people are carried along, obedient to environment; the wills and desires of others stronger than themselves; heredity; suggestion; and other outward causes moving them about like pawns on the Chessboard of Life. But the Masters, rising to the plane above, dominate their moods, characters, qualities, and powers, as well as the environment surrounding them, and become Movers instead of pawns. They help to PLAY THE GAME OF LIFE, instead of being played and moved about by other wills and environment. They USE the Principle instead of being its tools. The Masters obey the Causation of the higher planes, but they help to RULE on their own plane. In this statement there is condensed a wealth of Hermetic knowledge – let him read who can.

7. The Principle of Gender

"Gender is in everything; everything has its Masculine and Feminine Principles; Gender manifests on all planes." – The Kybalion.

This Principle embodies the truth that there is GENDER manifested in everything – the Masculine and Feminine Principles ever at work. This is true not only of the Physical Plane, but of the Mental and even the Spiritual Planes. On the Physical Plane, the Principle manifests as SEX, on the higher planes it takes higher forms, but the Principle is ever the same. No creation, physical, mental or spiritual, is possible without this Principle. An understanding of its laws will throw light on many a subject that has perplexed the minds of men. The Principle of Gender works ever in the direction of generation, regeneration, and creation. Everything, and every person, contains the two Elements or Principles, or this great Principle, within it, him or her. Every Male thing has the Female Element also; every Female contains also the Male Principle. If you would understand the philosophy of Mental and Spiritual Creation, Generation, and Re-generation, you must understand and study this Hermetic Principle. It contains the solution of many mysteries of Life. We caution you that this Principle has no reference to the many base, pernicious and degrading lustful theories, teachings and practices, which are taught under fanciful titles, and which are a prostitution of the great natural principle of Gender. Such base revivals of the ancient infamous forms of Phallicism tend to ruin mind, body and soul, and the Hermetic Philosophy has ever sounded the warning note against these degraded teachings which tend toward lust, licentiousness, and perversion of Nature's principles. If you seek such teachings, you must go elsewhere for them – Hermeticism contains nothing for you along these lines. To the pure, all things are pure; to the base, all things are base.

CHAPTER III

MENTAL TRANSMUTATION

"Mind (as well as metals and elements) may be transmuted, from state to state; degree to degree; condition to condition; pole to pole; vibration to vibration. True Hermetic Transmutation is a Mental Art." – The Kybalion.

As we have stated, the Hermetists were the original alchemists, astrologers, and psychologists, Hermes having been the founder of these schools of thought. From astrology has grown modern astronomy; from alchemy has grown modern chemistry; from the mystic psychology has grown the modern psychology of the schools. But it must not be supposed that the ancients were ignorant of that which the modern schools suppose to be their exclusive and special property. The records engraved on the stones of Ancient Egypt show conclusively that the ancients had a full comprehensive knowledge of astronomy, the very building of the Pyramids showing the connection between their design and the study of astronomical science. Nor were they ignorant of Chemistry, for the fragments of the ancient writings show that they were acquainted with the chemical properties of things; in fact, the ancient theories regarding physics are being slowly verified by the latest discoveries of modern science, notably those relating to the constitution of matter. Nor must it be supposed that they were ignorant of the so-called modern discoveries in psychology – on the contrary, the Egyptians were especially skilled in the science of Psychology, particularly in the branches that the modern schools ignore, but which, nevertheless, are being uncovered under the name of "psychic science" which is perplexing the psychologists of to-day, and making them reluctantly admit that "there may be something in it after all."

The truth is, that beneath the material chemistry, astronomy and psychology (that is, the psychology in its phase of "brain-action") the ancients possessed a knowledge of transcendental astronomy, called astrology; of transcendental chemistry, called alchemy; of transcendental psychology, called mystic psychology. They possessed the Inner Knowledge as well as the Outer Knowledge, the latter alone being possessed by modern scientists. Among the many secret branches of knowledge possessed by the Hermetists, was that known as Mental Transmutation, which forms the subject matter of this lesson.

"Transmutation" is a term usually employed to designate the ancient art of the transmutation of metals – particularly of the base metals into gold. The word "Transmute" means "to change from one nature, form, or substance, into another; to transform" (Webster). And accordingly, "Mental Transmutation" means the art of changing and transforming mental states, forms, and conditions, into others. So you may see that Mental Transmutation is the "Art of Mental Chemistry," if you like the term – a form of practical Mystic Psychology.

But this means far more than appears on the surface. Transmutation, Alchemy, or Chemistry on the Mental Plane is important enough in its effects, to be sure, and if the art stopped there it would still be one of the most important branches of study known to man. But this is only the beginning. Let us see why!

The first of the Seven Hermetic Principles is the Principle of Mentalism, the axiom of which is "THE ALL is Mind; the Universe is Mental," which means that the Underlying Reality of the Universe is Mind; and the Universe itself is Mental – that is, "existing in the Mind of THE ALL." We shall consider this Principle in succeeding lessons, but let us see the effect of the principle if it be assumed to be true.

If the Universe is Mental in its nature, then Mental Transmutation must be the art of CHANGING THE CONDITIONS OF THE UNIVERSE, along the lines of Matter, Force and mind. So you see, therefore, that Mental Transmutation is really the "Magic" of which the ancient writers had so much to say in their mystical works, and about which they gave so few practical instructions. If All be Mental, then the art which enables one to transmute mental conditions must render the Master the controller of material conditions as well as those ordinarily called "mental."

As a matter of fact, none but advanced Mental Alchemists have been able to attain the degree of power necessary to control the grosser physical conditions, such as the control of the elements of Nature; the production or cessation of tempests; the production and cessation of earthquakes and other great physical phenomena. But that such men have existed, and do exist today, is a matter of earnest belief to all advanced occultists of all schools. That the Masters exist, and have these powers, the best teachers assure their students, having had experiences which justify them in such belief and statements. These Masters do not make public exhibitions of their powers, but seek seclusion from the crowds of men, in order to better work their way along the Path of Attainment. We mention their existence, at this point, merely to call your attention to the fact that their power is entirely Mental, and operates along the lines of the higher Mental Transmutation, under the Hermetic Principle of Mentalism.

"The Universe is Mental" – The Kybalion.

But students and Hermetists of lesser degree than Masters – the Initiates and Teachers – are able to freely work along the Mental Plane, in Mental Transmutation. In fact all that we call "psychic phenomena,"; "mental influence"; "mental science"; "new-thought phenomena," etc., operates along the same general lines, for there is but one principle involved, no matter by what name the phenomena be called.

The student and practitioner of Mental Transmutation works among the Mental Plane, transmuting mental conditions, states, etc., into others, according to various formulas, more or less efficacious. The various "treatments," "affirmations," "denials" etc., of the schools of mental science are but formulas, often quite imperfect and unscientific, of The Hermetic Art. The majority of modern practitioners are quite ignorant compared to the ancient masters, for they lack the fundamental knowledge upon which the work is based.

Not only may the mental states, etc., of one's self be changed or transmuted by Hermetic Methods; but also the states of others may be, and are, constantly transmuted in the same way, usually unconsciously, but often consciously by some understanding the laws and principles, in cases where the people affected are not informed of the principles of self-protection. And more than this, as many students and practitioners of modern mental science know, every material condition depending upon the minds of other people may be changed or transmuted in accordance with the earnest desire, will, and "treatments" of person desiring changed conditions of life. The public are so generally informed regarding these things at present, that we do not deem it necessary to mention the same at length, our purpose at this point being merely to show the Hermetic Principle and Art underlying all of these various forms of practice, good and evil, for the force can be used in opposite directions according to the Hermetic Principles of Polarity.

In this little book we shall state the basic principles of Mental Transmutation, that all who read may grasp the Underlying Principles, and thus possess the Master-Key that will unlock the many doors of the Principle of Polarity.

We shall now proceed to a consideration of the first of the Hermetic Seven Principles – the Principle of Mentalism, in which is explained the truth that "THE ALL is Mind; the Universe is Mental," in the words of The Kybalion. We ask the close attention, and careful study of this great Principle, on the part of our students, for it is really the Basic Principle of the whole Hermetic Philosophy, and of the Hermetic Art of Mental Transmutation.

CHAPTER IV

THE ALL

"Under, and back of, the Universe of Time, Space and Change, is ever to be found The Substantial Reality – the Fundamental Truth."
– The Kybalion.

"Substance" means: "that which underlies all outward manifestations; the essence; the essential reality; the thing in itself," etc. "Substantial" means: "actually existing; being the essential element; being real," etc. "Reality" means: "the state of being real; true, enduring; valid; fixed; permanent; actual," etc.

Under and behind all outward appearances or manifestations, there must always be a Substantial Reality. This is the Law. Man considering the Universe, of which he is a unit, sees nothing but change in matter, forces, and mental states. He sees that nothing really IS, but that everything is BECOMING and CHANGING. Nothing stands still-everything is being born, growing, dying-the very instant a thing reaches its height, it begins to decline – the law of rhythm is in constant operation – there is no reality, enduring quality, fixity, or substantiality in anything – nothing is permanent but Change. He sees all things evolving from other things, and resolving into other things – constant action and reaction; inflow and outflow; building up and tearing down; creation and destruction; birth, growth and death. Nothing endures but Change. And if he be a thinking man, he realizes that all of these changing things must be but outward appearances or manifestations of some Underlying Power – some Substantial Reality.

All thinkers, in all lands and in all times, have assumed the necessity for postulating the existence of this Substantial Reality. All philosophies worthy of the name have been based upon this thought. Men have given to this Substantial Reality many names – some have called it by the term of Deity (under many titles). Others have called it "The Infinite and Eternal Energy" others have tried to call it "Matter" – but all have acknowledged its existence. It is self-evident; it needs no argument.

In these lessons we have followed the example of some of the world's greatest thinkers, both ancient and modern – the Hermetic. Masters – and have called this Underlying Power – this Substantial Reality – by the Hermetic name of "THE ALL," which term we consider the most comprehensive of the many terms applied by Man to THAT which transcends names and terms.

We accept and teach the view of the great Hermetic thinkers of all times, as well as of those illumined souls who have reached higher planes of being, both of whom assert that the inner nature of THE ALL is UNKNOWABLE. This must be so, for naught by THE ALL itself can comprehend its own nature and being.

The Hermetists believe and teach that THE ALL, "in itself," is and must ever be UNKNOWABLE. They regard all the theories, guesses and speculations of the theologians and metaphysicians regarding the inner nature of THE ALL, as but the childish efforts of mortal minds to grasp the secret of the Infinite. Such efforts have always failed and will always fail, from the very nature of the task. One pursuing such inquiries travels around and around in the labyrinth of thought, until he is lost to all sane reasoning, action or conduct, and is utterly unfitted for the work of life. He is like the squirrel which frantically runs around and around the circling treadmill wheel of his cage, traveling ever and yet reaching nowhere – at the end a prisoner still, and standing just where he started.

And still more presumptuous are those who attempt to ascribe to THE ALL the personality, qualities, properties, characteristics and attributes of themselves, ascribing to THE ALL the human emotions, feelings, and characteristics, even down to the pettiest qualities of mankind, such as jealousy, susceptibility to flattery and praise, desire for offerings and worship, and all the other survivals from the days of the childhood of the race. Such ideas are not worthy of grown men and women, and are rapidly being discarded.

(At this point, it may be proper for me to state that we make a distinction between Religion and Theology – between Philosophy and Metaphysics. Religion, to us, means that intuitional realization of the existence of THE ALL, and one's relationship to it; while Theology means the attempts of men to ascribe personality, qualities, and characteristics to it; their theories regarding its affairs, will, desires, plans, and designs, and their assumption of the office of '' middlemen'' between THE ALL and the people. Philosophy, to us, means the inquiry after knowledge of things knowable and thinkable; while Metaphysics means the attempt to carry the inquiry over and beyond the boundaries and into regions unknowable and unthinkable, and with the same tendency as that of Theology. And consequently, both Religion and Philosophy mean to us things having roots in Reality, while Theology and Metaphysics seem like broken reeds, rooted in the quicksands of ignorance, and affording naught but the most insecure support for the mind or soul of Man. (We do not insist upon our students accepting these definitions – we mention them merely to show our position. At any rate, you shall hear very little about Theology and Metaphysics in these lessons.)

But while the essential nature of THE ALL is Unknowable, there are certain truths connected with its existence which the human mind finds itself compelled to accept. And an examination of these reports form a proper subject of inquiry, particularly as they agree with the reports of the Illumined on higher planes. And to this inquiry we now invite you.

"That which is the Fundamental Truth – the Substantial Reality – is beyond true naming, but the Wise Men call it THE ALL." – The Kybalion.

"In its Essence, THE ALL is UNKNOWABLE." – The Kybalion.

"But, the report of Reason must be hospitably received, and treated with respect." – The Kybalion.

The human reason, whose reports we must accept so long as we think at all, informs us as follows regarding THE ALL, and that without attempting to remove the veil of the Unknowable:

(1) THE ALL must be ALL that REALLY IS. There can be nothing existing outside of THE ALL, else THE ALL would not be THE ALL.

(2) THE ALL must be INFINITE, for there is nothing else to define, confine, bound, limit; or restrict THE ALL. It must be Infinite in Time, or ETERNAL, – it must have always continuously existed, for there is nothing else to have ever created it, and something can never evolve from nothing, and if it had ever "not been," even for a moment, it would not "be" now, – it must continuously exist forever, for there is nothing to destroy it, and it can never "not-be," even for a moment, because something can never become nothing. It must be Infinite in Space – it must be Everywhere, for there is no place outside of THE ALL – it cannot be otherwise than continuous in Space, without break, cessation, separation, or interruption, for there is nothing to break, separate, or interrupt its continuity, and nothing with which to "fill in the gaps." It must be Infinite in Power, or Absolute, for there is nothing to limit, restrict, restrain, confine, disturb or condition it – it is subject to no other Power, for there is no other Power.

(3) THE ALL must be IMMUTABLE, or not subject to change in its real nature, for there is nothing to work changes upon it nothing into which it could change, nor from which it could have changed. It cannot be added to nor subtracted from; increased nor diminished; nor become greater or lesser in any respect whatsoever. It must have always been, and must always remain, just what it is now – THE ALL – there has never been, is not now, and never will be, anything else into which it can change.

THE ALL being Infinite, Absolute, Eternal and Unchangeable it must follow that anything finite, changeable, fleeting, and conditioned cannot be THE ALL. And as there is Nothing outside of THE ALL, in Reality, then any and all such finite things must be as Nothing in Reality. Now do not become befogged, nor frightened – we are not trying to lead you into the Christian Science field under cover of Hermetic Philosophy. There is a Reconciliation of this apparently contradictory state of affairs. Be patient, we will reach it in time.

We see around us that which is called "Matter," which forms the physical foundation for all forms. Is THE ALL merely Matter? Not at all! Matter cannot manifest Life or Mind, and as Life and Mind are manifested in the Universe, THE ALL cannot be Matter, for nothing rises higher than its own source – nothing is ever manifested in an effect that is not in the cause – nothing is evolved as a consequent that is not involved as an antecedent. And then Modern Science informs us that there is really no such thing as Matter – that what we call Matter is merely "interrupted energy or force," that is, energy or force at a low rate of vibration. As a recent writer has said "Matter has melted into Mystery." Even Material Science has abandoned the theory of Matter, and now rests on the basis of "Energy."

Then is THE ALL mere Energy or Force? Not Energy or Force as the materialists use the terms, for their energy and force are blind, mechanical things, devoid of Life or Mind. Life and Mind can never evolve from blind Energy or Force, for the reason given a moment ago: "Nothing can rise higher than its source – nothing is evolved unless it is involved – nothing manifests in the effect, unless it is in the cause. " And so THE ALL cannot be mere Energy or Force, for, if it were, then there would be no such things as Life and Mind in existence, and we know better than that, for we are Alive and using Mind to consider this very question, and so are those who claim that Energy or Force is Everything.

What is there then higher than Matter or Energy that we know to be existent in the Universe? LIFE AND MIND! Life and Mind in all their varying degrees of unfoldment! "Then," you ask, "do you mean to tell us that THE ALL is LIFE and MIND?" Yes! and No! is our answer. If you mean Life and Mind as we poor petty mortals know them, we say No! THE ALL is not that! "But what kind of Life and Mind do you mean?" you ask.

The answer is "LIVING MIND," as far above that which mortals know by those words, as Life and Mind are higher than mechanical forces, or matter – INFINITE LIVING MIND as compared to finite "Life and Mind." We mean that which the illumined souls mean when they reverently pronounce the word: "SPIRIT!"

"THE ALL" is Infinite Living Mind – the Illumined call it SPIRIT!

CHAPTER V

THE MENTAL UNIVERSE

"The Universe is Mental – held in the Mind of THE ALL."

– The Kybalion.

THE ALL is SPIRIT! But what is Spirit? This question cannot be answered, for the reason that its definition is practically that of THE ALL, which cannot be explained or defined. Spirit is simply a name that men give to the highest conception of Infinite Living Mind – it means "the Real Essence" – it means Living Mind, as much superior to Life and Mind as we know them, as the latter are superior to mechanical Energy and Matter. Spirit transcends our understanding, and we use the term merely that we may think or speak of THE ALL. For the purposes of thought and understanding, we are justified in thinking of Spirit as Infinite Living Mind, at the same time acknowledging that we cannot fully understand it. We must either do this or stop thinking of the matter at all.

Let us now proceed to a consideration of the nature of the Universe, as a whole and in its parts. What is the Universe? We have seen that there can be nothing outside of THE ALL. Then is the Universe THE ALL? No, this cannot be, because the Universe seems to be made up of MANY, and is constantly changing, and in other ways it does not measure up to the ideas that we are compelled to accept regarding THE ALL, as stated in our last lesson. Then if the Universe be not THE ALL, then it must be Nothing – such is the inevitable conclusion of the mind at first thought. But this will not satisfy the question, for we are sensible of the existence of the Universe. Then if the Universe is neither THE ALL, nor Nothing, what Can it be? Let us examine this question.

If the Universe exists at all, or seems to exist, it must proceed in some way from THE ALL – it must be a creation of THE ALL. But as something can never come from nothing, from what could THE ALL have created it. Some philosophers have answered this question by saying that THE ALL created the Universe from ITSELF – that is, from the being and substance of THE ALL. But this will not do, for THE ALL cannot be subtracted from, nor divided, as we have seen, and then again if this be so, would not each particle in the Universe be aware of its being THE ALL – THE ALL could not lose its knowledge of itself, nor actually BECOME an atom, or blind force, or lowly living thing. Some men, indeed, realizing that THE ALL is indeed ALL, and also recognizing that they, the men, existed, have jumped to the conclusion that they and THE ALL were identical, and they have filled the air with shouts of "I AM GOD," to the amusement of the multitude and the sorrow of sages. The claim of the corpuscle that: "I am Man!" would be modest in comparison.

But, what indeed is the Universe, if it be not THE ALL, not yet created by THE ALL having separated itself into fragments? What else can it be – of what else can it be made? This is the great question. Let us examine it carefully. We find here that the "Principle of Correspondence" (see Lesson I.) comes to our aid here. The old Hermetic axiom, "As above so below," may be pressed into service at this point. Let us endeavor to get a glimpse of the workings on higher planes by examining those on our own. The Principle of Correspondence must apply to this as well as to other problems.

Let us see! On his own plane of being, how does Man create? Well, first, he may create by making something out of outside materials. But this will not do, for there are no materials outside of THE ALL with which it may create. Well, then, secondly, Man pro-creates or reproduces his kind by the process of begetting, which is self-multiplication accomplished by transferring a portion of his substance to his offspring. But this will not do, because THE ALL cannot transfer or subtract a portion of itself, nor can it reproduce or multiply itself – in the first place there would be a taking away, and in the second case a multiplication or addition to THE ALL, both thoughts being an absurdity. Is there no third way in which MAN creates? Yes, there is – he CREATES MENTALLY! And in so doing he uses no outside materials, nor does he reproduce himself, and yet his Spirit pervades the Mental Creation.

Following the Principle of Correspondence, we are justified in considering that THE ALL creates the Universe MENTALLY, in a manner akin to the process whereby Man creates Mental Images. And, here is where the report of Reason tallies precisely with the report of the Illumined, as shown by their teachings and writings. Such are the teachings of the Wise Men. Such was the Teaching of Hermes.

THE ALL can create in no other way except mentally, without either using material (and there is none to use), or else reproducing itself (which is also impossible). There is no escape from this conclusion of the Reason, which, as we have said, agrees with the highest teachings of the Illumined. Just as you, student, may create a Universe of your own in your mentality, so does THE ALL create Universes in its own Mentality. But your Universe is the mental creation of a Finite Mind, whereas that of THE ALL is the creation of an Infinite. The two are similar in kind, but infinitely different in degree. We shall examine more closely into the process of creation and manifestation as we proceed. But this is the point to fix in your minds at this stage: THE UNIVERSE, AND ALL IT CONTAINS, IS A MENTAL CREATION OF THE ALL. Verily indeed, ALL IS MIND!

"THE ALL creates in its Infinite Mind countless Universes, which exist for aeons of Time – and yet, to THE ALL, the creation, development, decline and death of a million Universes is as the time of the twinkling of an eye."

– The Kybalion.

"The Infinite Mind of THE ALL is the womb of Universes."

– The Kybalion.

The Principle of Gender (see Lesson I. and other lessons to follow) is manifested on all planes of life, material mental and spiritual. But, as we have said before, "Gender" does not mean "Sex" sex is merely a material manifestation of gender. "Gender" means "relating to generation or creation." And whenever anything is generated or created, on any plane, the Principle of Gender must be manifested. And this is true even in the creation of Universes.

Now do not jump to the conclusion that we are teaching that there is a male and female God, or Creator. That idea is merely a distortion of the ancient teachings on the subject. The true teaching is that THE ALL, in itself, is above Gender, as it is above every other Law, including those of Time and Space. It is the Law, from which the Laws proceed, and it is not subject to them. But when THE ALL manifests on the plane of generation or creation, then it acts according to Law and Principle, for it is moving on a lower plane of Being. And consequently it manifests the Principle of Gender, in its Masculine and Feminine aspects, on the Mental Plane, of course.

This idea may seem startling to some of you who hear it for the first time, but you have all really passively accepted it in your everyday conceptions. You speak of the Fatherhood of God, and the Motherhood of Nature – of God, the Divine Father, and Nature the Universal Mother – and have thus instinctively acknowledged the Principle of Gender in the Universe. Is this not so?

But, the Hermetic teaching does not imply a real duality – THE ALL is ONE – the Two Aspects are merely aspects of manifestation. The teaching is that The Masculine Principle manifested by THE ALL stands, in a way, apart from the actual mental creation of the Universe. It projects its Will toward the Feminine Principle (which may be called "Nature") whereupon the latter begins the actual work of the evolution of the Universe, from simple "centers of activity" on to man, and then on and on still higher, all according to well-established and firmly enforced Laws of Nature. If you prefer the old figures of thought, you may think of the Masculine Principle as GOD, the Father, and of the Feminine Principle as NATURE, the Universal Mother, from whose womb all things have been born. This is more than a mere poetic figure of speech – it is an idea of the actual process of the creation of the Universe. But always remember, that THE ALL is but One, and that in its Infinite Mind the Universe is generated, created and exists.

It may help you to get the proper idea, if you will apply the Law of Correspondence to yourself, and your own mind. You know that the part of You which you call "I," in a sense, stands apart and witnesses the creation of mental Images in your own mind. The part of your mind in which the mental generation is accomplished may be called the "Me" in distinction from the "I" which stands apart and witnesses and examines the thoughts, ideas and images of the "Me." "As above, so below," remember, and the phenomena of one plane may be employed to solve the riddles of higher or lower planes.

Is it any wonder that You, the child, feel that instinctive reverence for THE ALL, which feeling we call "religion" – that respect, and reverence for THE FATHER MIND? Is it any wonder that, when you consider the works and wonders of Nature, you are overcome with a mighty feeling which has its roots away down in your inmost being? It is the MOTHER MIND that you are pressing close up to, like a babe to the breast.

Do not make the mistake of supposing that the little world you see around you – the Earth, which is a mere grain of dust in the Universe – is the Universe itself. There are millions upon millions of such worlds, and greater. And there are millions of millions of such Universes in existence within the Infinite Mind of THE ALL. And even in our own little solar system there are regions and planes of life far higher than ours, and beings compared to which we earth-bound mortals are as the slimy life-forms that dwell on the ocean's bed when compared to Man. There are beings with powers and attributes higher than Man has ever dreamed of the gods' possessing. And yet these beings were once as you, and still lower – and you will be even as they, and still higher, in time, for such is the Destiny of Man as reported by the Illumined.

And Death is not real, even in the Relative sense – it is but Birth to a new life – and You shall go on, and on, and on, to higher and still higher planes of life, for aeons upon aeons of time. The Universe is your home, and you shall explore its farthest recesses before the end of Time. You are dwelling in the Infinite Mind of THE ALL, and your possibilities and opportunities are infinite, both in time and space. And at the end of the Grand Cycle of Aeons, when THE ALL shall draw back into itself all of its creations – you will go gladly for you will then be able to know the Whole Truth of being At One with THE ALL. Such is the report of the Illumined – those who have advanced well along The Path.

And, in the meantime, rest calm and serene – you are safe and protected by the Infinite Power of the FATHER-MOTHER MIND.

"*Within the Father-Mother Mind, mortal children are at home.*"
– The Kybalion.

"*There is not one who is Fatherless, nor Motherless in the Universe.*"
– The Kybalion.

CHAPTER VI

THE DIVINE PARADOX

"The half-wise, recognizing the comparative unreality of the Universe, imagine that they may defy its Laws – such are vain and presumptuous fools, and they are broken against the rocks and torn asunder by the elements by reason of their folly. The truly wise, knowing the nature of the Universe, use Law against laws; the higher against the lower; and by the Art of Alchemy transmute that which is undesirable into that which is worthy, and thus triumph. Mastery consists not in abnormal dreams, visions and fantastic imaginings or living, but in using the higher forces against the lower – escaping the pains of the lower planes by vibrating on the higher. Transmutation, not presumptuous denial, is the weapon of the Master." – The Kybalion.

This is the Paradox of the Universe, resulting from the Principle of Polarity which manifests when THE ALL begins to Create – hearken to it for it points the difference between half-wisdom and wisdom. While to THE INFINITE ALL, the Universe, its Laws, its Powers, its life, its Phenomena, are as things witnessed in the state of Meditation or Dream; yet to all that is Finite, the Universe must be treated as Real, and life, and action, and thought, must be based thereupon, accordingly, although with an ever understanding of the Higher Truth. Each according to its own Plane and Laws. Were THE ALL to imagine that the Universe were indeed Reality, then woe to the Universe, for there would be then no escape from lower to higher, divineward – then would the Universe become a fixity and progress would become impossible. And if Man, owing to half-wisdom, acts and lives and thinks of the Universe as merely a dream (akin to his own finite dreams) then indeed does it so become for him, and like a sleep-walker he stumbles ever around and around in a circle, making no progress, and being forced into an awakening at last by his falling bruised and bleeding over the Natural Laws which he ignored. Keep your mind ever on the Star, but let your eyes watch over your footsteps, lest you fall into the mire by reason of your upward gaze. Remember the Divine Paradox, that while the Universe IS NOT, still IT IS. Remember ever the Two Poles of Truth the Absolute and the Relative. Beware of Half-Truths.

What Hermetists know as "the Law of Paradox" is an aspect of the Principle of Polarity. The Hermetic writings are filled with references to the appearance of the Paradox in the consideration of the problems of Life and Being. The Teachers are constantly warning their students against the error of omitting the "other side" of any question. And their warnings are particularly directed to the problems of the Absolute and the Relative, which perplex all students of philosophy, and which cause so many to think and act contrary to what is generally known as "common sense." And we caution all students to be sure to grasp the Divine Paradox of the Absolute and Relative, lest they become entangled in the mire of the Half-Truth. With this in view this particular lesson has been written. Read it carefully!

The first thought that comes to the thinking man after he realizes the truth that the Universe is a Mental Creation of THE ALL, is that the Universe and all that it contains is a mere illusion; an unreality; against which idea his instincts revolt. But this, like all other great truths, must be considered both from the Absolute and the Relative points of view. From the Absolute viewpoint, of course, the Universe is in the nature of an illusion, a dream, a phantasmagoria, as compared to THE ALL in itself. We recognize this even in our ordinary view, for we speak of the world as "a fleeting show" that comes and goes, is born and dies – for the element of impermanence and change, finiteness and unsubstantiality, must ever be connected with the idea of a created Universe when it is contrasted with the idea of THE ALL, no matter what may be our beliefs concerning the nature of both. Philosopher, metaphysician, scientist and theologian all agree upon this idea, and the thought is found in all forms of philosophical thought and religious conceptions, as well as in the theories of the respective schools of metaphysics and theology.

So, the Hermetic Teachings do not preach the unsubstantiality of the Universe in any stronger terms than those more familiar to you, although their presentation of the subject may seem somewhat more startling. Anything that has a beginning and an ending must be, in a sense, unreal and untrue, and the Universe comes under the rule, in all schools of thought. From the Absolute point of view, there is nothing Real except THE ALL, no matter what terms we may use in thinking of, or discussing the subject. Whether the Universe be created of Matter, or whether it be a Mental Creation in the Mind of THE ALL – it is unsubstantial, non-enduring, a thing of time, space and change. We want you to realize this fact thoroughly, before you pass judgment on the Hermetic conception of the Mental nature of the Universe. Think over any and all of the other conceptions, and see whether this be not true of them.

But the Absolute point of view shows merely one side of the picture – the other side is the Relative one. Absolute Truth has been defined as "Things as the mind of God knows them," while Relative Truth is "Things as the highest reason of Man understands them." And so while to THE ALL the Universe must be unreal and illusionary, a mere dream or result of meditation, – nevertheless, to the finite minds forming a part of that Universe, and viewing it through mortal faculties, the Universe is very real indeed, and must be so considered. In recognizing the Absolute view, we must not make the mistake of ignoring or denying the facts and phenomena of the Universe as they present themselves to our mortal faculties – we are not THE ALL, remember.

To take familiar illustrations, we all recognize the fact that matter "exists" to our senses – we will fare badly if we do not. And yet, even our finite minds understand the scientific dictum that there is no such thing as Matter from a scientific point of view – that which we call Matter is held to be merely an aggregation of atoms, which atoms themselves are merely a grouping of units of force, called electrons or "ions," vibrating and in constant circular motion. We kick a stone and we feel the impact – it seems to be real, notwithstanding that we know it to be merely what we have stated above. But remember that our foot, which feels the impact by means of our brains, is likewise Matter, so constituted of electrons, and for that matter so are our brains. And, at the best, if it were not by reason of our Mind, we would not know the foot or stone at all.

Then again, the ideal of the artist or sculptor, which he is endeavoring to reproduce in stone or on canvas, seems very real to him. So do the characters in the mind of the author; or dramatist, which he seeks to express so that others may recognize them. And if this be true in the case of our finite minds, what must be the degree of Reality in the Mental Images created in the Mind of the Infinite? Oh, friends, to mortals this Universe of Mentality is very real indeed – it is the only one we can ever know, though we rise from plane to plane, higher and higher in it. To know it otherwise, but actual experience, we must be THE ALL itself. It is true that the higher we rise in the scale – the nearer to "the mind of the Father" we reach – the more apparent becomes the illusory nature of finite things, but not until THE ALL finally withdraws us into itself does the vision actually vanish.

So, we need not dwell upon the feature of illusion. Rather let us, recognizing the real nature of the Universe, seek to understand its mental laws, and endeavor to use them to the best effect in our upward progress through life, as we travel from plane to plane of being. The Laws of the Universe are none the less "Iron Laws" in spite of their mental nature. All, except THE ALL, are bound by them. What is IN THE INFINITE MIND OF THE ALL is REAL in a degree second only to that Reality itself which is vested in the nature of THE ALL.

So, do not feel insecure or afraid – we are all HELD FIRMLY IN THE INFINITE MIND OF THE ALL, and there is naught to hurt us or for us to fear. There is no Power outside of THE ALL to affect us. So we may rest calm and secure. There is a world of comfort and security in this realization when once attained. Then "calm and peaceful do we sleep, rocked in the Cradle of the Deep" – resting safely on the bosom of the Ocean of Infinite Mind, which is THE ALL. In THE ALL, indeed, do "we live and move and have our being."

Matter is none the less Matter to us, while we dwell on the plane of Matter, although we know it to be merely an aggregation of "electrons," or particles of Force, vibrating rapidly and gyrating around each other in the formations of atoms; the atoms in turn vibrating and gyrating, forming molecules, which latter in turn form larger masses of Matter. Nor does Matter become less Matter, when we follow the inquiry still further, and learn from the Hermetic Teachings, that the "Force" of which the electrons are but units is merely a manifestation of the Mind of THE ALL, and like all else in the Universe is purely Mental in its nature. While on the Plane of matter, we must recognize its phenomena – we may control Matter (as all Masters of higher or lesser degree do), but we do so by applying the higher forces. We commit a folly when we attempt to deny the existence of Matter in the relative aspect. We may deny its mastery over us – and rightly so – but we should not attempt to ignore it in its relative aspect, at least so long as we dwell upon its plane.

Nor do the Laws of Nature become less constant or effective, when we know them, likewise, to be merely mental creations. They are in full effect on the various planes. We overcome the lower laws, by applying still higher ones – and in this way only. But we cannot escape Law or rise above it entirely. Nothing but THE ALL can escape Law – and that because THE ALL is LAW itself, from which all Laws emerge. The most advanced Masters may acquire the powers usually attributed to the gods of men; and there are countless ranks of being, in the great hierarchy of life, whose being and power transcends even that of the highest Masters among men to a degree unthinkable by mortals, but even the highest Master, and the highest Being, must bow to the Law, and be as Nothing in the eye of THE ALL. So that if even these highest Beings, whose powers exceed even those attributed by men to their gods – if even these are bound by and are subservient to Law, then imagine the presumption of mortal man, of our race and grade, when he dares to consider the Laws of Nature as "unreal!" visionary and illusory, because he happens to be able to grasp the truth that the Laws are Mental in nature, and simply Mental Creations of THE ALL. Those Laws which THE ALL intends to be governing Laws are not to be defied or argued away. So long as the Universe endures, will they endure – for the Universe exists by virtue of these Laws which form its framework and which hold it together.

The Hermetic Principle of Mentalism, while explaining the true nature of the Universe upon the principle that all is Mental, does not change the scientific conceptions of the Universe, Life, or Evolution. In fact, science merely corroborates the Hermetic Teachings. The latter merely teaches that the nature of the Universe is "Mental," while modern science has taught that it is "Material"; or (of late) that it is "Energy" at the last analysis. The Hermetic Teachings have no fault to find with Herbert Spencer's basic principle which postulates the existence of an "Infinite and Eternal Energy, from which all things proceed." In fact, the Hermetics recognize in Spencer's philosophy the highest outside statement of the workings of the Natural Laws that have ever been promulgated, and they believe Spencer to have been a reincarnation of an ancient philosopher who dwelt in ancient Egypt thousands of years ago, and who later incarnated as Heraclitus, the Grecian philosopher who lived B. C. 500. And they regard his statement of the "Infinite and Eternal Energy" as directly in the line of the Hermetic Teachings, always with the addition of their own doctrine that his "Energy" is the Energy of the Mind of THE ALL. With the Master-Key of the Hermetic Philosophy, the student of Spencer will be able to unlock many doors of the inner philosophical conceptions of the great English philosopher, whose work shows the results of the preparation of his previous incarnations. His teachings regarding Evolution and Rhythm are in almost perfect agreement with the Hermetic Teachings regarding the Principle of Rhythm.

So, the student of Hermetics need not lay aside any of his cherished scientific views regarding the Universe. All he is asked to do is to grasp the underlying principle of "THE ALL is Mind; the Universe is Mental – held in the mind of THE ALL." He will find that the other six of the Seven Principles will "fit into" his scientific knowledge, and will serve to bring out obscure points and to throw light in dark corners. This is not to be wondered at, when we realize the influence of the Hermetic thought of the early philosophers of Greece, upon whose foundations of thought the theories of modern science largely rest. The acceptance of the First Hermetic Principle (Mentalism) is the only great point of difference between Modern Science and Hermetic students, and Science is gradually moving toward the Hermetic position in its groping in the dark for a way out of the Labyrinth into which it has wandered in its search for Reality.

The purpose of this lesson is to impress upon the minds of our students the fact that, to all intents and purposes, the Universe and its laws, and its phenomena, are just as REAL, so far as Man is concerned, as they would be under the hypotheses of Materialism or Energism. Under any hypothesis the Universe in its outer aspect is changing, ever-flowing, and transitory – and therefore devoid of substantiality and reality. But (note the other pole of the truth) under the same hypotheses, we are compelled to ACT AND LIVE as if the fleeting things were real and substantial. With this difference, always, between the various hypotheses – that under the old views Mental Power was ignored as a Natural Force, while under Mentalism it becomes the Greatest Natural Force. And this one difference revolutionizes Life, to those who understand the Principle and its resulting laws and practice.

So, finally, students all, grasp the advantage of Mentalism, and learn to know, use and apply the laws resulting therefrom. But do not yield to the temptation which, as The Kybalion states, overcomes the half-wise and which causes them to be hypnotized by the apparent unreality of things, the consequence being that they wander about like dream-people dwelling in a world of dreams, ignoring the practical work and life of man, the end being that "they are broken against the rocks and torn asunder by the elements, by reason of their folly." Rather follow the example of the wise, which the same authority states, "use Law against Laws; the higher against the lower; and by the Art of Alchemy transmute that which is undesirable into that which is worthy, and thus triumph." Following the authority, let us avoid the half-wisdom (which is folly) which ignores the truth that: "Mastery consists not in abnormal dreams, visions, and fantastic imaginings or living, but in using the higher forces against the lower – escaping the pains of the lower planes by vibrating on the higher." Remember always, student, that "Transmutation, not presumptuous denial, is the weapon of the Master." The above quotations are from The Kybalion, and are worthy of being committed to memory by the student.

We do not live in a world of dreams, but in an Universe which while relative, is real so far as our lives and actions are concerned. Our business in the Universe is not to deny its existence, but to LIVE, using the Laws to rise from lower to higher – living on, doing the best that we can under the circumstances arising each day, and living, so far as is possible, to our biggest ideas and ideals. The true Meaning of Life is not known to men on this plane if, indeed, to any – but the highest authorities, and our own intuitions, teach us that we will make no mistake in living up to the best that is in us, so far as is possible, and realising the Universal tendency in the same direction in spite of apparent evidence to the contrary. We are all on The Path – and the road leads upward ever, with frequent resting places.

Read the message of The Kybalion – and follow the example of "the wise" – avoiding the mistake of "the half-wise" who perish by reason of their folly.

CHAPTER VII

"THE ALL" IN ALL

"While All is in THE ALL, it is equally true that THE ALL is in All. To him who truly understands this truth hath come great knowledge." – The Kybalion.

How often have the majority of people heard repeated the statement that their Deity (called by many names) was "All in All" and how little have they suspected the inner occult truth concealed by these carelessly uttered words? The commonly used expression is a survival of the ancient Hermetic Maxim quoted above. As the Kybalion says: "To him who truly understands this truth, hath come great knowledge." And, this being so, let us seek this truth, the understanding of which means so much. In this statement of truth – this Hermetic Maxim – is concealed one of the greatest philosophical, scientific and religious truths.

We have given you the Hermetic Teaching regarding the Mental Nature of the Universe – the truth that "the Universe is Mental – held in the Mind of THE ALL." As the Kybalion says, in the passage quoted above: "All is in THE ALL." But note also the co-related statement, that: "It is equally true that THE ALL is in ALL." This apparently contradictory statement is reconcilable under the Law of Paradox. It is, moreover, an exact Hermetic statement of the relations existing between THE ALL and its Mental Universe. We have seen how "All is in THE ALL" – now let us examine the other aspect of the subject.

The Hermetic Teachings are to the effect that THE ALL is Imminent in ("remaining within; inherent; abiding within") its Universe, and in every part, particle, unit, or combination, within the Universe. This statement is usually illustrated by the Teachers by a reference to the Principle of Correspondence. The Teacher instructs the student to form a Mental Image of something, a person, an idea, something having a mental form, the favorite example being that of the author or dramatist forming an idea of his characters; or a painter or sculptor forming an image of an ideal that he wishes to express by his art. In each case, the student will find that while the image has its existence, and being, solely within his own mind, yet he, the student, author, dramatist, painter, or sculptor, is, in a sense, immanent in; remaining within; or abiding within, the mental image also. In other words, the entire virtue, life, spirit, of reality in the mental image is derived from the "immanent mind" of the thinker. Consider this for a moment, until the idea is grasped.

To take a modern example, let us say that Othello, Iago, Hamlet, Lear, Richard III, existed merely in the mind of Shakespeare, at the time of their conception or creation. And yet, Shakespeare also existed within each of these characters, giving them their vitality, spirit, and action. Whose is the "spirit" of the characters that we know as Micawber, Oliver Twist, Uriah Heep – is it Dickens, or have each of these characters a personal spirit, independent of their creator? Have the Venus of Medici, the Sistine Madonna, the Apollo Belvidere, spirits and reality of their own, or do they represent the spiritual and mental power of their creators?

The Law of Paradox explains that both propositions are true, viewed from the proper viewpoints. Micawber is both Micawber, and yet Dickens. And, again, while Micawber may be said to be Dickens, yet Dickens is not identical with Micawber. Man, like Micawber, may exclaim: "The Spirit of my Creator is inherent within me – and yet I am not HE!" How different this from the shocking half-truth so vociferously announced by certain of the half-wise, who fill the air with their raucous cries of: "I am God!" Imagine poor Micawber, or the sneaky Uriah Heep, crying: "I Am Dickens"; or some of the lowly clods in one of Shakespeare's plays, eloquently announcing that: "I Am Shakespeare!"

THE ALL is in the earthworm, and yet the earth-worm is far from being THE ALL. And still the wonder remains, that though the earth-worm exists merely as a lowly thing, created and having its being solely within the Mind of THE ALL – yet THE ALL is immanent in the earthworm, and in the particles that go to make up the earth-worm. Can there be any greater mystery than this of "All in THE ALL; and THE ALL in All?"

The student will, of course, realize that the illustrations given above are necessarily imperfect and inadequate, for they represent the creation of mental images in finite minds, while the Universe is a creation of Infinite Mind – and the difference between the two poles separates them. And yet it is merely a matter of degree – the same Principle is in operation – the Principle of Correspondence manifests in each – "As above, so Below; as Below, so above."

And, in the degree that Man realizes the existence of the Indwelling Spirit immanent within his being, so will he rise in the spiritual scale of life. This is what spiritual development means – the recognition, realization, and manifestation of the Spirit within us.

Try to remember this last definition – that of spiritual development. It contains the Truth of True Religion.

There are many planes of Being – many sub-planes of Life – many degrees of existence in the Universe. And all depend upon the advancement of beings in the scale, of which scale the lowest point is the grossest matter, the highest being separated only by the thinnest division from the SPIRIT of THE ALL. And, upward and onward along this Scale of Life, everything is moving. All are on the Path, whose end is THE ALL. All progress is a Returning Home. All is Upward and Onward, in spite of all seemingly contradictory appearances. Such is the message of the Illumined.

The Hermetic Teachings concerning the process of the Mental Creation of the Universe, are that at the beginning of the Creative Cycle, THE ALL, in its aspect of Being, projects its Will toward its aspect of "Becoming" and the process of creation begins. It is taught that the process consists of the lowering of Vibration until a very low degree of vibratory energy is reached, at which point the grossest possible form of Matter is manifested. This process is called the stage of Involution, in which THE ALL becomes "involved," or "wrapped up," in its creation. This process is believed by the Hermetists to have a Correspondence to the mental process of an artist, writer, or inventor, who becomes so wrapped up in his mental creation as to almost forget his own existence and who, for the time being, almost "lives in his creation," If instead of "wrapped" we use the word "rapt," perhaps we will give a better idea of what is meant.

This Involuntary stage of Creation is sometimes called the "Outpouring" of the Divine Energy, just as the Evolutionary state is called the "Indrawing." The extreme pole of the Creative process is considered to be the furthest removed from THE ALL, while the beginning of the Evolutionary stage is regarded as the beginning of the return swing of the pendulum of Rhythm – a "coming home" idea being held in all of the Hermetic Teachings.

The Teachings are that during the "Outpouring," the vibrations become lower and lower until finally the urge ceases, and the return swing begins. But there is this difference, that while in the "Outpouring" the creative forces manifest compactly and as a whole, yet from the beginning of the Evolutionary or "Indrawing" stage, there is manifested the Law of Individualization – that is, the tendency to separate into Units of Force, so that finally that which left THE ALL as unindividualized energy returns to its source as countless highly developed Units of Life, having risen higher and higher in the scale by means of Physical, Mental and Spiritual Evolution.

The ancient Hermetists use the word "Meditation" in describing the process of the mental creation of the Universe in the Mind of THE ALL, the word "Contemplation" also being frequently employed. But the idea intended seems to be that of the employment of the Divine Attention. "Attention" is a word derived from the Latin root, meaning "to reach out; to stretch out," and so the act of Attention is really a mental "reaching out; extension" of mental energy, so that the underlying idea is readily understood when we examine into the real meaning of "Attention."

The Hermetic Teachings regarding the process of Evolution are that, THE ALL, having meditated upon the beginning of the Creation – having thus established the material foundations of the Universe – having thought it into existence – then gradually awakens or rouses from its Meditation and in so doing starts into manifestation the process of Evolution, on the material mental and spiritual planes, successively and in order. Thus the upward movement begins – and all begins to move Spiritward. Matter becomes less gross; the Units spring into being; the combinations begin to form; Life appears and manifests in higher and higher forms; and Mind becomes more and more in evidence – the vibrations constantly becoming higher. In short, the entire process of Evolution, in all of its phases, begins, and proceeds according to the established "Laws of the Indrawing" process. All of this occupies aeons upon aeons of Man's time, each aeon containing countless millions of years, but yet the Illumined inform us that the entire creation, including Involution and Evolution, of an Universe, is but "as the twinkle of the eye" to THE ALL. At the end of countless cycles of aeons of time, THE ALL withdraws its Attention – its Contemplation and Meditation – of the Universe, for the Great Work is finished – and All is withdrawn into THE ALL from which it emerged. But Mystery of Mysteries – the Spirit of each soul is not annihilated, but is infinitely expanded – the Created and the Creator are merged. Such is the report of the Illumined!

The above illustration of the "meditation," and subsequent "awakening from meditation," of THE ALL, is of course but an attempt of the teachers to describe the Infinite process by a finite example. And, yet: "As Below, so Above." The difference is merely in degree. And just as THE ALL arouses itself from the meditation upon the Universe, so does Man (in time) cease from manifesting upon the Material Plane, and withdraws himself more and more into the Indwelling Spirit, which is indeed "The Divine Ego."

There is one more matter of which we desire to speak in this lesson, and that comes very near to an invasion of the Metaphysical field of speculation, although our purpose is merely to show the futility of such speculation. We allude to the question which inevitably comes to the mind of all thinkers who have ventured to seek the Truth. The question is: "WHY does THE ALL create Universes" The question may be asked in different forms, but the above is the gist of the inquiry.

Men have striven hard to answer this question, but still there is no answer worthy of the name. Some have imagined that THE ALL had something to gain by it, but this is absurd, for what could THE ALL gain that it did not already possess? Others have sought the answer in the idea that THE ALL "wished something to love" and others that it created for pleasure, or amusement; or because it "was lonely" or to manifest its power; – all puerile explanations and ideas, belonging to the childish period of thought.

Others have sought to explain the mystery by assuming that THE ALL found itself "compelled" to create, by reason of its own "internal nature" – its "creative instinct." This idea is in advance of the others, but its weak point lies in the idea of THE ALL being "compelled" by anything, internal or external. If its "internal nature," or "creative instinct," compelled it to do anything, then the "internal nature" or "creative instinct" would be the Absolute, instead of THE ALL, and so accordingly that part of the proposition falls. And, yet, THE ALL does create and manifest, and seems to find some kind of satisfaction in so doing. And it is difficult to escape the conclusion that in some infinite degree it must have what would correspond to an "inner nature," or "creative instinct," in man, with correspondingly infinite Desire and Will. It could not act unless it Willed to Act; and it would not Will to Act, unless it Desired to Act and it would not Desire to Act unless it obtained some Satisfaction thereby. And all of these things would belong to an "Inner Nature," and might be postulated as existing according to the Law of Correspondence. But, still, we prefer to think of THE ALL as acting entirely FREE from any influence, internal as well as external. That is the problem which lies at the root of the difficulty – and the difficulty that lies at the root of the problem.

Strictly speaking, there cannot be said to be any "Reason" whatsoever for THE ALL to act, for a "reason" implies a "cause," and THE ALL is above Cause and Effect, except when it Wills to become a Cause, at which time the Principle is set into motion. So, you see, the matter is Unthinkable, just as THE ALL is Unknowable. Just as we say THE ALL merely "IS" – so we are compelled to say that "THE ALL ACTS BECAUSE IT ACTS." At the last, THE ALL is All Reason in Itself; All Law in Itself; All Action in Itself – and it may be said, truthfully, that THE ALL is Its Own Reason; its own Law; its own Act – or still further, that THE ALL; Its Reason; Its Act; is Law; are ONE, all being names for the same thing. In the opinion of those who are giving you these present lessons, the answer is locked up in the INNER SELF of THE ALL, along with its Secret of Being. The Law of Correspondence, in our opinion, reaches only to that aspect of THE ALL, which may be spoken of as "The Aspect of BECOMING." Back of that Aspect is "The Aspect of BEING" in which all Laws are lost in LAW; all Principles merge into PRINCIPLE – and THE ALL; PRINCIPLE; and BEING; are IDENTICAL, ONE AND THE SAME. Therefore, Metaphysical speculation on this point is futile. We go into the matter here, merely to show that we recognize the question, and also the absurdity of the ordinary answers of metaphysics and theology.

In conclusion, it may be of interest to our students to learn that while some of the ancient, and modern, Hermetic Teachers have rather inclined in the direction of applying the Principle of Correspondence to the question, with the result of the "Inner Nature" conclusion, – still the legends have it that HERMES, the Great, when asked this question by his advanced students, answered them by PRESSING HIS LIPS TIGHTLY TOGETHER and saying not a word, indicating that there WAS NO ANSWER. But, then, he may have intended to apply the axiom of his philosophy, that: "The lips of Wisdom are closed, except to the ears of Understanding," believing that even his advanced students did not possess the

Understanding which entitled them to the Teaching. At any rate, if Hermes possessed the Secret, he failed to impart it, and so far as the world is concerned THE LIPS OF HERMES ARE CLOSED regarding it. And where the Great Hermes hesitated to speak, what mortal may dare to teach?

But, remember, that whatever be the answer to this problem, if indeed there be an answer the truth remains that: "While All is in THE ALL, it is equally true that THE ALL is in All." The Teaching on this point is emphatic. And, we may add the concluding words of the quotation: "To him who truly understands this truth, hath come great knowledge."

CHAPTER VIII
PLANES OF CORRESPONDENCE

"As above, so below; as below, so above." – The Kybalion.

The great Second Hermetic Principle embodies the truth that there is a harmony, agreement, and correspondence between the several planes of Manifestation, Life and Being. This truth is a truth because all that is included in the Universe emanates from the same source, and the same laws, principles, and characteristics apply to each unit, or combination of units, of activity, as each manifests its own phenomena upon its own plane.

For the purpose of convenience of thought and study, the Hermetic Philosophy considers that the Universe may be divided into three great classes of phenomena, known as the Three Great Planes, namely:

1. The Great Physical Plane.
2. The Great Mental Plane.
3. The Great Spiritual Plane.

These divisions are more or less artificial and arbitrary, for the truth is that all of the three divisions are but ascending degrees of the great scale of Life, the lowest point of which is undifferentiated Matter, and the highest point that of Spirit. And, moreover, the different Planes shade into each other, so that no hard and fast division may be made between the higher phenomena of the Physical and the lower of the Mental; or between the higher of the Mental and the lower of the Physical.

In short, the Three Great Planes may be regarded as three great groups of degrees of Life Manifestation. While the purposes of this little book do not allow us to enter into an extended discussion of, or explanation of, the subject of these different planes, still we think it well to give a general description of the same at this point.

At the beginning we may as well consider the question so often asked by the neophyte, who desires to be informed regarding the meaning of the word "Plane", which term has been very freely used, and very poorly explained, in many recent works upon the subject of occultism. The question is generally about as follows: "Is a Plane a place having dimensions, or is it merely a condition or state?" We answer: "No, not a place, nor ordinary dimension of space; and yet more than a state or condition. It may be considered as a state or condition, and yet the state or condition is a degree of dimension, in a scale subject to measurement."

Somewhat paradoxical, is it not? But let us examine the matter. A "dimension," you know, is "a measure in a straight line, relating to measure," etc. The ordinary dimensions of space are length, breadth, and height, or perhaps length, breadth, height, thickness or circumference. But there is another dimension of "created things" or "measure in a straight line," known to occultists, and to scientists as well, although the latter have not as yet applied the term "dimension" to it – and this new dimension, which, by the way, is the much speculated-about "Fourth Dimension," is the standard used in determining the degrees or "planes."

This Fourth Dimension may be called "The Dimension of Vibration" It is a fact well known to modern science, as well as to the Hermetists who have embodied the truth in their "Third Hermetic Principle," that "everything is in motion; everything vibrates; nothing is at rest." From the highest manifestation, to the lowest, everything and all things Vibrate. Not only do they vibrate at different rates of motion, but as in different directions and in a different manner. The degrees of the rate of vibrations constitute the degrees of measurement on the Scale of Vibrations – in other words the degrees of the Fourth Dimension. And these degrees form what occultists call "Planes" The higher the degree of rate of vibration, the higher the plane, and the higher the manifestation of Life occupying that plane. So that while a plane is not "a place," nor yet "a state or condition," yet it possesses qualities common to both. We shall have more to say regarding the subject of the scale of Vibrations in our next lessons, in which we shall consider the Hermetic Principle of Vibration.

You will kindly remember, however, that the Three Great Planes are not actual divisions of the phenomena of the Universe, but merely arbitrary terms used by the Hermetists in order to aid in the thought and study of the various degrees and Forms of universal activity and life. The atom of matter, the unit of force, the mind of man, and the being of the arch-angel are all but degrees in one scale, and all fundamentally the same, the difference between solely a matter of degree, and rate of vibration – all are creations of THE ALL, and have their existence solely within the Infinite Mind of THE ALL.

The Hermetists sub-divide each of the Three Great Planes into Seven Minor Planes, and each of these latter are also sub-divided into seven sub-planes, all divisions being more or less arbitrary, shading into each other, and adopted merely for convenience of scientific study and thought.

The Great Physical Plane, and its Seven Minor Planes, is that division of the phenomena of the Universe which includes all that relates to physics, or material things, forces, and manifestations. It includes all forms of that which we call Matter, and all forms of that which we call Energy or Force. But you must remember that the Hermetic Philosophy does not recognize Matter as a thing in itself, or as having a separate existence even in the Mind of THE ALL. The

Teachings are that Matter is but a form of Energy – .that is, Energy at a low rate of vibrations of a certain kind. And accordingly the Hermetists classify Matter under the head of Energy, and give to it three of the Seven Minor Planes of the Great Physical Plane.

These Seven Minor Physical Planes are as follows:

1. The Plane of Matter (A)
2. The Plane of Matter (B)
3. The Plane of Matter (C)
4. The Plane of Ethereal Substance
5. The Plane of Energy (A)
6. The Plane of Energy (B)
7. The Plane of Energy (C)

The Plane of Matter (A) comprises the forms of Matter in its form of solids, liquids, and gases, as generally recognized by the text-books on physics. The Plane of Matter (B) comprises certain higher and more subtle forms of Matter of the existence of which modern science is but now recognizing, the phenomena of Radiant Matter, in its phases of radium, etc., belonging to the lower sub-division of this Minor Plane. The Plane of Matter (C) comprises forms of the most subtle and tenuous Matter, the existence of which is not suspected by ordinary scientists. The Plane of Ethereal Substance comprises that which science speaks of as "The Ether", a substance of extreme tenuity and elasticity, pervading all Universal Space, and acting as a medium for the transmission of waves of energy, such as light, heat, electricity, etc. This Ethereal Substance forms a connecting link between Matter (so-called) and Energy, and partakes of the nature of each. The Hermetic Teachings, however, instruct that this plane has seven sub-divisions (as have all of the Minor Planes), and that in fact there are seven ethers, instead of but one.

Next above the Plane of Ethereal Substance comes the Plane of Energy (A), which comprises the ordinary forms of Energy known to science, its seven sub-planes being, respectively, Heat; Light; Magnetism; Electricity, and Attraction (including Gravitation, Cohesion, Chemical Affinity, etc.) and several other forms of energy indicated by scientific experiments but not as yet named or classified. The Plane of Energy (B) comprises seven subplanes of higher forms of energy not as yet discovered by science, but which have been called "Nature's Finer Forces" and which are called into operation in manifestations of certain forms of mental phenomena, and by which such phenomena becomes possible. The Plane of Energy (C) comprises seven sub-planes of energy so highly organized that it bears many of the characteristics of "life," but which is not recognized by the minds of men on the ordinary plane of development, being available for the use on beings of the Spiritual Plane alone – such energy is unthinkable to ordinary man, and may be considered almost as "the divine power." The beings employing the same are as "gods" compared even to the highest human types known to us.

The Great Mental Plane comprises those forms of "living things" known to us in ordinary life, as well as certain other forms not so well known except to the occultist. The classification of the Seven Minor Mental Planes is more or less satisfactory and arbitrary (unless accompanied by elaborate explanations which are foreign to the purpose of this particular work), but we may as well mention them. They are as follows:

1. The Plane of Mineral Mind
2. The Plane of Elemental Mind (A)
3. The Plane of Plant Mind
4. The Plane of Elemental Mind (B)
5. The Plane of Animal Mind
6. The Plane of Elemental Mind (C)
7. The Plane of Human Mind

The Plane of Mineral Mind comprises the "states or conditions" of the units or entities, or groups and combinations of the same, which animate the forms known to us as "minerals, chemicals, etc." These entities must not be confounded with the molecules, atoms and corpuscles themselves, the latter being merely the material bodies or forms of these entities, just as a man's body is but his material form and not "himself." These entities may be called "souls" in one sense, and are living beings of a low degree of development, life, and mind – just a little more than the units of "living energy" which comprise the higher sub-divisions of the highest Physical Plane. The average mind does not generally attribute the possession of mind, soul, or life, to the mineral kingdom, but all occultists recognize the existence of the same, and modern science is rapidly moving forward to the point-of-view of the Hermetic, in this respect. The molecules, atoms and corpuscles have their "loves and hates"; "likes and dislikes"; "attractions and repulsions"; "affinities and non-affinities," etc., and some of the more daring of modern scientific minds have expressed the opinion that the desire and will, emotions and feelings, of the atoms differ only in degree from those of men. We have no time or space to argue this matter here. All occultists know it to be a fact, and others are referred to some of the more recent scientific works for outside corroboration. There are the usual seven sub-divisions to this plane.

The Plane of Elemental Mind (A) comprises the state or condition, and degree of mental and vital development of a class of entities unknown to the average man, but recognized to occultists. They are invisible to the ordinary senses of man, but, nevertheless, exist and play their part of the Drama of the Universe. Their degree of intelligence is between that of the mineral and chemical entities on the one hand, and of the entities of the plant kingdom on the other. There are seven subdivisions to this plane, also.

The Plane of Plant Mind, in its seven sub-divisions, comprises the states or conditions of the entities comprising the kingdoms of the Plant World, the vital and mental phenomena of which is fairly well understood by the average intelligent person, many new and interesting scientific works regarding "Mind and Life in Plants" having been published during the last decade. Plants have life, mind and "souls," as well as have the animals, man, and super-man.

The Plane of Elemental Mind (B), in its seven sub-divisions, comprises the states and conditions of a higher form of "elemental" or unseen entities, playing their part in the general work of the Universe, the mind and life of which form a part of the scale between the Plane of Plant Mind and the Plane of Animal Mind, the entities partaking of the nature of both.

The Plane of Animal Mind, in its seven sub-divisions, comprises the states and conditions of the entities, beings, or souls, animating the animal forms of life, familiar to us all. It is not necessary to go into details regarding this kingdom or plane of life, for the animal world is as familiar to us as is our own.

The Plane of Elemental Mind (C), in its seven sub-divisions, comprises those entities or beings, invisible as are all such elemental forms, which partake of the nature of both animal and human life in a degree and in certain combinations. The highest forms are semi-human in intelligence.

The Plane of Human Mind, in its seven sub-divisions, comprises those manifestations of life and mentality which are common to Man, in his various grades, degrees, and divisions. In this connection, we wish to point out the fact that the average man of today occupies but the fourth sub-division of the Plane of Human Mind, and only the most intelligent have crossed the borders of the Fifth Sub-Division. It has taken the race millions of years to reach this stage, and it will take many more years for the race to move on to the sixth and seventh sub-divisions, and beyond. But, remember, that there have been races before us which have passed through these degrees, and then on to higher planes. Our own race is the fifth (with stragglers from the fourth) which has set foot upon The Path. And, then there are a few advanced souls of our own race who have outstripped the masses, and who have passed on to the sixth and seventh sub-division, and some few being still further on. The man of the Sixth Sub-Division will be "The Super-Man"; he of the Seventh will be "The Over-Man."

In our consideration of the Seven Minor Mental Planes, we have merely referred to the Three Elementary Planes in a general way. We do not wish to go into this subject in detail in this work, for it does not belong to this part of the general philosophy and teachings. But we may say this much, in order to give you a little clearer idea, of the relations of these planes to the more familiar ones – the Elementary Planes bear the same relation to the Planes of Mineral, Plant, Animal and Human Mentality and Life, that the black keys on the piano do to the white keys. The white keys are sufficient to produce music, but there are certain scales, melodies, and harmonies, in which the black keys play their part, and in which their presence is necessary. They are also necessary as "connecting links" of soul-condition; entity states, etc., between the several other planes, certain forms of development being attained therein – this last fact giving to the reader who can "read between the lines" a new light upon the processes of Evolution, and a new key to the secret door of the "leaps of life" between kingdom and kingdom. The great kingdoms of Elementals are fully recognized by all occultists, and the esoteric writings are full of mention of them. The readers of Bulwer's "Zanoni" and similar tales will recognize the entities inhabiting these planes of life.

Passing on from the Great Mental Plane to the Great Spiritual Plane, what shall we say? How can we explain these higher states of Being, Life and Mind, to minds as yet unable to grasp and understand the higher subdivisions of the Plane of Human Mind? The task is impossible. We can speak only in the most general terms. How may Light be described to a man born blind – how sugar, to a man who has never tasted anything sweet – how harmony, to one born deaf?

All that we can say is that the Seven Minor Planes of the Great Spiritual Plane (each Minor Plane having its seven sub-divisions) comprise Beings possessing Life, Mind and Form as far above that of Man of to-day as the latter is above the earth-worm, mineral or even certain forms of Energy or Matter. The Life of these Beings so far transcends ours, that we cannot even think of the details of the same; their minds so far transcend ours, that to them we scarcely seem to "think," and our mental processes seem almost akin to material processes; the Matter of which their forms are composed is of the highest Planes of Matter, nay, some are even said to be "clothed in Pure Energy." What may be said of such Beings?

On the Seven Minor Planes of the Great Spiritual Plane exist Beings of whom we may speak as Angels; Archangels; Demi-Gods. On the lower Minor Planes dwell those great souls whom we call Masters and Adepts. Above them come the Great Hierarchies of the Angelic Hosts, unthinkable to man; and above those come those who may without irreverence be called "The Gods," so high in the scale of Being are they, their being, intelligence and power being akin to those attributed by the races of men to their conceptions of Deity. These Beings are beyond even the highest flights of the human imagination, the word "Divine" being the only one applicable to them. Many of these Beings, as well as the Angelic Host, take the greatest interest in the affairs of the Universe and play an important part in its affairs. These Unseen Divinities and Angelic Helpers extend their influence freely and powerfully, in the process of Evolution, and Cosmic Progress. Their occasional intervention and assistance in human affairs have led to the many legends, beliefs, religions and traditions of the race, past and present. They have superimposed their knowledge and power upon the world, again and again, all under the Law of THE ALL, of course.

But, yet, even the highest of these advanced Beings exist merely as creations of, and in, the Mind of THE ALL, and are subject to the Cosmic Processes and Universal Laws. They are still Mortal. We may call them "gods" if we like, but still they are but the Elder Brethren of the Race, – the advanced souls who have outstripped their brethren, and who have foregone the ecstasy of Absorption by THE ALL, in order to help the race on its upward journey along The Path. But, they belong to the Universe, and are subject to its conditions – they are mortal – and their plane is below that of Absolute Spirit.

Only the most advanced Hermetists are able to grasp the Inner Teachings regarding the state of existence, and the powers manifested on the Spiritual Planes. The phenomena is so much higher than that of the Mental Planes that a confusion of ideas would surely result from an attempt to describe the same. Only those whose minds have been carefully trained along the lines of the Hermetic Philosophy for years – yes, those who have brought with them from other incarnations the knowledge acquired previously – can comprehend just what is meant by the Teaching regarding these Spiritual Planes. And much of these Inner Teachings is held by the Hermetists as being too sacred, important and even dangerous for general public dissemination. The intelligent student may recognize what we mean by this when we state that the meaning of "Spirit" as used by the Hermetists is akin to "Living Power"; "Animated Force;" "Inner Essence;" "Essence of Life," etc., which meaning must not be confounded with that usually and commonly employed in connection with the term, i.e., "religious; ecclesiastical; spiritual; ethereal; holy," etc., etc. To occultists the word "Spirit" is used in the sense of "The Animating Principle," carrying with it the idea of Power, Living Energy, Mystic Force, etc. And occultists know that that which is known to them as "Spiritual Power" may be employed for evil as well as good ends (in accordance with the Principle of Polarity), a fact which has been recognized by the majority of religions in their conceptions of Satan, Beelzebub, the Devil, Lucifer, Fallen Angels, etc. And so the knowledge regarding these Planes has been kept in the Holy of Holies in all Esoteric Fraternities and Occult Orders, – in the Secret Chamber of the Temple. But this may be said here, that those who have attained high spiritual powers and have misused them, have a terrible fate in store for them, and the swing of the pendulum of Rhythm will inevitably swing them back to the furthest extreme of Material existence, from which point they must retrace their steps Spiritward, along the weary rounds of The Path, but always with the added torture of having always with them a lingering memory of the heights from which they fell owing to their evil actions. The legends of the Fallen Angels have a basis in actual facts, as all advanced occultists know. The striving for selfish power on the Spiritual Planes inevitably results in the selfish soul losing its spiritual balance and falling back as far as it had previously risen. But to even such a soul, the opportunity of a return is given – and such souls make the return journey, paying the terrible penalty according to the invariable Law.

In conclusion we would again remind you that according to the Principle of Correspondence, which embodies the truth: "As Above so Below; as Below, so Above," all of the Seven Hermetic Principles are in full operation on all of the many planes, Physical Mental and Spiritual.

The Principle of Mental Substance of course applies to all the planes, for all are held in the Mind of THE ALL.

The Principle of Correspondence manifests in all, for there is a correspondence, harmony and agreement between the several planes.

The Principle of Vibration manifests on all planes, in fact the very differences that go to make the "planes" arise from Vibration, as we have explained.

The Principle of Polarity manifests on each plane, the extremes of the Poles being apparently opposite and contradictory.

The Principle of Rhythm manifests on each Plane, the movement of the phenomena having its ebb and flow, rise and flow, incoming and outgoing.

The Principle of Cause and Effect manifests on each Plane, every Effect having its Cause and every Cause having its effect.

The Principle of Gender manifests on each Plane, the Creative Energy being always manifest, and operating along the lines of its Masculine and Feminine Aspects.

"As Above so Below; as Below, so Above." This centuries old Hermetic axiom embodies one of the great Principles of Universal Phenomena. As we proceed with our consideration of the remaining Principles, we will see even more clearly the truth of the universal nature of this great Principle of Correspondence.

CHAPTER IX

VIBRATION

"Nothing rests; everything moves; everything vibrates." – The Kybalion.

The great Third Hermetic Principle – the Principle of Vibration – embodies the truth that Motion is manifest in everything in the Universe – that nothing is at rest – that everything moves, vibrates, and circles. This Hermetic Principle was recognized by some of the early Greek philosophers who embodied it in their systems. But, then, for centuries it was lost sight of by the thinkers outside of the Hermetic ranks. But in the Nineteenth Century physical science re-discovered the truth and the Twentieth Century scientific discoveries have added additional proof of the correctness and truth of this centuries-old Hermetic doctrine.

The Hermetic Teachings are that not only is everything in constant movement and vibration, but that the "differences" between the various manifestations of the universal power are due entirely to the varying rate and mode of vibrations. Not only this, but that even THE ALL, in itself, manifests a constant vibration of such an infinite degree of intensity and rapid motion that it may be practically considered as at rest, the teachers directing the attention of the students to the fact that even on the physical plane a rapidly moving object (such as a revolving wheel) seems to be at rest. The Teachings are to the effect that Spirit is at one end of the Pole of Vibration, the other Pole being certain extremely gross forms of Matter. Between these two poles are millions upon millions of different rates and modes of vibration.

Modern Science has proven that all that we call Matter and Energy are but "modes of vibratory motion," and some of the more advanced scientists are rapidly moving toward the positions of the occultists who hold that the phenomena of Mind are likewise modes of vibration or motion. Let us see what science has to say regarding the question of vibrations in matter and energy.

In the first place, science teaches that all matter manifests, in some degree, the vibrations arising from temperature or heat. Be an object cold or hot – both being but degrees of the same things – it manifests certain heat vibrations, and in that sense is in motion and vibration. Then all particles of Matter are in circular movement, from corpuscle to suns. The planets revolve around suns, and many of them turn on their axes. The suns move around greater central points, and these are believed to move around still greater, and so on, ad infinitum. The molecules of which the particular kinds of Matter are composed are in a state of constant vibration and movement around each other and against each other. The molecules are composed of Atoms, which, likewise, are in a state of constant movement and vibration. The atoms are composed of Corpuscles, sometimes called "electrons," "ions," etc., which also are in a state of rapid motion, revolving around each other, and which manifest a very rapid state and mode of vibration. And, so we see that all forms of Matter manifest Vibration, in accordance with the Hermetic Principle of Vibration.

And so it is with the various forms of Energy. Science teaches that Light, Heat, Magnetism and Electricity are but forms of vibratory motion connected in some way with, and probably emanating from the Ether. Science does not as yet attempt to explain the nature of the phenomena known as Cohesion, which is the principle of Molecular Attraction; nor Chemical Affinity, which is the principle of Atomic Attraction; nor Gravitation (the greatest mystery of the three), which is the principle of attraction by which every particle or mass of Matter is bound to every other particle or mass. These three forms of Energy are not as yet understood by science, yet the writers incline to the opinion that these too are manifestations of some form of vibratory energy, a fact which the Hermetists have held and taught for ages past.

The Universal Ether, which is postulated by science without its nature being understood clearly, is held by the Hermetists to be but a higher manifestation of that which is erroneously called matter – that is to say, Matter at a higher degree of vibration – and is called by them "The Ethereal Substance." The Hermetists teach that this Ethereal Substance is of extreme tenuity and elasticity, and pervades universal space, serving as a medium of transmission of waves of vibratory energy, such as heat, light, electricity, magnetism, etc. The Teachings are that The Ethereal Substance is a connecting link between the forms of vibratory energy known as "Matter" on the one hand, and "Energy or Force" on the other; and also that it manifests a degree of vibration, in rate and mode, entirely its own.

Scientists have offered the illustration of a rapidly moving wheel, top, or cylinder, to show the effects of increasing rates of vibration. The illustration supposes a wheel, top, or revolving cylinder, running at a low rate of speed – we will call this revolving thing "the object" in following out the illustration. Let us suppose the object is moving slowly. It may be seen readily, but no sound of its movement reaches the ear. The speed is gradually increased. In a few moments its movement becomes so rapid that a deep growl or low note may be heard. Then as the rate is increased the note rises one in the musical scale. Then, the motion being still further increased, the next highest note is distinguished. Then, one after another, all the notes of the musical scale appear, rising higher and higher as the motion is increased. Finally when the motions have reached a certain rate the final note perceptible to human ears is reached and the shrill, piercing shriek dies away, and silence follows. No sound is heard from the revolving object, the rate of motion being so high that the human ear cannot register the vibrations. Then comes the perception of rising degrees of Heat. Then after quite a time the eye catches a glimpse of the object becoming a dull dark reddish color. As the rate increases, the red becomes brighter. Then as the speed is increased, the red melts into an orange. Then the orange melts into a yellow. Then follow, successively, the shades of green, blue, indigo, and finally violet, as the rate of sped increases. Then the violet shades away, and all color disappears, the human eye not being able to register them. But there are invisible rays emanating from the revolving object, the rays that are used in photographing, and other subtle rays of light. Then begin to manifest the peculiar rays known as the "X Rays," etc., as the constitution of the object changes. Electricity and Magnetism are emitted when the appropriate rate of vibration is attained.

When the object reaches a certain rate of vibration its molecules disintegrate, and resolve themselves into the original elements or atoms. Then the atoms, following the Principle of Vibration, are separated into the countless corpuscles of which they are composed. And finally, even the corpuscles disappear and the object may be said to be composed of The Ethereal Substance. Science does not dare to follow the illustration further, but the Hermetists teach that if the vibrations be continually increased the object would mount up the successive states of manifestation and would in turn manifest the various mental stages, and then on Spiritward, until it would finally re-enter THE ALL, which is Absolute Spirit. The "object," however, would have ceased to be an "object" long before the stage of Ethereal Substance was reached, but otherwise the illustration is correct inasmuch as it shows the effect of constantly increased rates and modes of vibration. It must be remembered, in the above illustration, that at the stages at which the "object" throws off vibrations of light, heat, etc., it is not actually "resolved" into those forms of energy (which are much higher in the scale), but simply that it reaches a degree of vibration in which those forms of energy are liberated, in a degree, from the confining influences of its molecules, atoms and corpuscles, as the case may be. These forms of energy, although much higher in the scale than matter, are imprisoned and confined in the material combinations, by reason of the energies manifesting through, and using material forms, but thus becoming entangled and confined in their creations of material forms, which, to an extent, is true of all creations, the creating force becoming involved in its creation.

But the Hermetic Teachings go much further than do those of modern science. They teach that all manifestation of thought, emotion, reason, will or desire, or any mental state or condition, are accompanied by vibrations, a portion of which are thrown off and which tend to affect the minds of other persons by "induction." This is the principle which produces the phenomena of "telepathy"; mental influence, and other forms of the action and power of mind over mind, with which the general public is rapidly becoming acquainted, owing to the wide dissemination of occult knowledge by the various schools, cults and teachers along these lines at this time.

Every thought, emotion or mental state has its corresponding rate and mode of vibration. And by an effort of the will of the person, or of other persons, these mental states may be reproduced, just as a musical tone may be reproduced by causing an instrument to vibrate at a certain rate – just as color may be reproduced in the same may. By a knowledge of the Principle of Vibration, as applied to Mental Phenomena, one may polarize his mind at any degree he wishes, thus gaining a perfect control over his mental states, moods, etc. In the same way he may affect the minds of others, producing the desired mental states in them. In short, he may be able to produce on the Mental Plane that which science produces on the Physical Plane – namely, "Vibrations at Will." This power of course may be acquired only by the proper instruction, exercises, practice, etc., the science being that of Mental Transmutation, one of the branches of the Hermetic Art.

A little reflection on what we have said will show the student that the Principle of Vibration underlies the wonderful phenomena of the power manifested by the Masters and Adepts, who are able to apparently set aside the Laws of Nature, but who, in reality, are simply using one law against another; one principle against others; and who accomplish their results by changing the vibrations of material objects, or forms of energy, and thus perform what are commonly called "miracles."

As one of the old Hermetic writers has truly said: "He who understands the Principle of Vibration, has grasped the scepter of Power."

CHAPTER X

POLARITY

"Everything is dual; everything has poles; everything has its pair of opposites; like and unlike are the same; opposites are identical in nature, but different in degree; extremes meet; all truths are but half-truths; all paradoxes may be reconciled." – The Kybalion.

The great Fourth Hermetic Principle – the Principle of Polarity – embodies the truth that all manifested things have "two sides"; "two aspects"; "two poles"; a "pair of opposites," with manifold degrees between the two extremes. The old paradoxes, which have ever perplexed the mind of men, are explained by an understanding of this Principle. Man has always recognized something akin to this Principle, and has endeavored to express it by such sayings, maxims and aphorisms as the following: "Everything is and isn't, at the same time"; "all truths are but half-truths"; "every truth is half-false"; "there are two sides to everything" – "there is a reverse side to every shield," etc., etc.

The Hermetic Teachings are to the effect that the difference between things seemingly diametrically opposed to each other is merely a matter of degree. It teaches that "the pairs of opposites may be reconciled," and that "thesis and antithesis are identical in nature, but different in degree"; and that the "universal reconciliation of opposites" is effected by a recognition of this Principle of Polarity. The teachers claim that illustrations of this Principle may be had on every hand, and from an examination into the real nature of anything. They begin by showing that Spirit and Matter are but the two poles of the same thing, the intermediate planes being merely degrees of vibration. They show that THE ALL and The Many are the same, the difference being merely a matter of degree of Mental Manifestation. Thus the LAW and Laws are the two opposite poles of one thing. Likewise, PRINCIPLE and Principles. Infinite Mind and finite minds.

Then passing on to the Physical Plane, they illustrate the Principle by showing that Heat and Cold are identical in nature, the differences being merely a matter of degrees. The thermometer shows many degrees of temperature, the lowest pole being called "cold," and the highest "heat." Between these two poles are many degrees of "heat" or "cold," call them either and you are equally correct. The higher of two degrees is always "warmer," while the lower is always "colder." There is no absolute standard – all is a matter of degree. There is no place on the thermometer where heat ceases and cold begins. It is all a matter of higher or lower vibrations. The very terms "high" and "low," which we are compelled to use, are but poles of the same thing – the terms are relative. So with "East and West" – travel around the world in an eastward direction, and you reach a point which is called west at your starting point, and you return from that westward point. Travel far enough North, and you will find yourself traveling South, or vice versa.

Light and Darkness are poles of the same thing, with many degrees between them. The musical scale is the same – starting with "C" you move upward until you reach another "C" and so on, the differences between the two ends of the board being the same, with many degrees between the two extremes. The scale of color is the same – higher and lower vibrations being the only difference between high violet and low red. Large and Small are relative. So are Noise and Quiet; Hard and Soft follow the rule. Likewise Sharp and Dull. Positive and Negative are two poles of the same thing, with countless degrees between them.

Good and Bad are not absolute – we call one end of the scale Good and the other Bad, or one end Good and the other Evil, according to the use of the terms. A thing is "less good" than the thing higher in the scale; but that "less good" thing, in turn, is "more good" than the thing next below it – and so on, the "more or less" being regulated by the position on the scale.

And so it is on the Mental Plane. "Love and. Hate" are generally regarded as being things diametrically opposed to each other; entirely different; unreconcilable. But we apply the Principle of Polarity; we find that there is no such thing as Absolute Love or Absolute Hate, as distinguished from each other. The two are merely terms applied to the two poles of the same thing. Beginning at any point of the scale we find "more love," or "less hate," as we ascend the scale; and "more hate" or "less love" as we descend this being true no matter from what point, high or low, we may start. There are degrees of Love and Hate, and there is a middle point where "Like and Dislike" become so faint that it is difficult to distinguish between them. Courage and Fear come under the same rule. The Pairs of Opposites exist everywhere. Where you find one thing you find its opposite – the two poles.

And it is this fact that enables the Hermetist to transmute one mental state into another, along the lines of Polarization. Things belonging to different classes cannot be transmuted into each other, but things of the same class may be changed, that is, may have their polarity changed. Thus Love never becomes East or West, or Red or Violet – but it may and often does turn into Hate and likewise Hate may be transformed into Love, by changing its polarity. Courage may be transmuted into Fear, and the reverse. Hard things may be rendered Soft. Dull things become Sharp. Hot things become Cold. And so on, the transmutation always being between things of the same kind of different degrees. Take the case of a Fearful man. By raising his mental vibrations along the line of Fear-

Courage, he can be filled with the highest degree of Courage and Fearlessness. And, likewise, the Slothful man may change himself into an Active, Energetic individual simply by polarizing along the lines of the desired quality.

The student who is familiar with the processes by which the various schools of Mental Science, etc., produce changes in the mental states of those following their teachings, may not readily understand the principle underlying many of these changes. When, however, the Principle of Polarity is once grasped, and it is seen that the mental changes are occasioned by a change of polarity – a sliding along the same scale – the matter is readily understood. The change is not in the nature of a transmutation of one thing into another thing entirely different – but is merely a change of degree in the same things, a vastly important difference. For instance, borrowing an analogy from the Physical Plane, it is impossible to change Heat into Sharpness, Loudness, Highness, etc., but Heat may readily be transmuted into Cold, simply by lowering the vibrations. In the same way Hate and Love are mutually transmutable; so are Fear and Courage. But Fear cannot be transformed into Love, nor can Courage be transmuted into Hate. The mental states belong to innumerable classes, each class of which has its opposite poles, along which transmutation is possible.

The student will readily recognize that in the mental states, as well as in the phenomena of the Physical Plane, the two poles may be classified as Positive and Negative, respectively. Thus Love is Positive to Hate; Courage to Fear; Activity to Non-Activity, etc., etc. And it will also be noticed that even to those unfamiliar with the Principle of Vibration, the Positive pole seems to be of a higher degree than the Negative, and readily dominates it. The tendency of Nature is in the direction of the dominant activity of the Positive pole.

In addition to the changing of the poles of one's own mental states by the operation of the art of Polarization, the phenomena of Mental Influence, in its manifold phases, shows us that the principle may be extended so as to embrace the phenomena of the influence of one mind over that of another, of which so much has been written and taught of late years. When it is understood that Mental Induction is possible, that is, that mental states may be produced by "induction" from others, then we can readily see how a certain rate of vibration, or polarization of a certain mental state, may be communicated to another person, and his polarity in that class of mental states thus changed. It is along this principle that the results of many of the "mental treatments" are obtained. For instance, a person is "blue," melancholy and full of fear. A mental scientist bringing his own mind up to the desired vibration by his trained will, and thus obtaining the desired polarization in his own case, then produces a similar mental state in the other by induction, the result being that the vibrations are raised and the person polarizes toward the Positive end of the scale instead toward the

Negative, and his Fear and other negative emotions are transmuted to Courage and similar positive mental states. A little study will show you that these mental changes are nearly all along the line of Polarization, the change being one of degree rather than of kind.

A knowledge of the existence of this great Hermetic Principle will enable the student to better understand his own mental states, and those of other people. He will see that these states are all matters of degree, and seeing thus, he will be able to raise or lower the vibration at will – to change his mental poles, and thus be Master of his mental states, instead of being their servant and slave. And by his knowledge he will be able to aid his fellows intelligently and by the appropriate methods change the polarity when the same is desirable. We advise all students to familiarize themselves with this Principle of Polarity, for a correct understanding of the same will throw light on many difficult subjects.

CHAPTER XI

RHYTHM

"Everything flows out and in; everything has its tides; all things rise and fall; the pendulum-swing manifests in everything; the measure of the swing to the right, is the measure of the swing to the left; rhythm compensates" – The Kybalion.

The great Fifth Hermetic Principle – the Principle of Rhythm – embodies the truth that in everything there is manifested a measured motion; a to-and-from movement; a flow and inflow; a swing forward and backward; a pendulum-like movement; a tide-like ebb and flow; a high-tide and a low-tide; between the two poles manifest on the physical, mental or spiritual planes. The Principle of rhythm is closely connected with the Principle of Polarity described in the preceding chapter. Rhythm manifests between the two poles established by the Principle of Polarity. This does not mean, however, that the pendulum of Rhythm swings to the extreme poles, for this rarely happens; in fact, it is difficult to establish the extreme polar opposites in the majority of cases. But the swing is ever "toward" first one pole and then the other.

There is always an action and reaction; an advance and a retreat; a rising and a sinking; manifested in all of the airs and phenomena of the Universe. Suns, worlds, men, animals, plants, minerals, forces, energy, mind and matter, yes, even Spirit, manifests this Principle. The Principle manifests in the creation and destruction of worlds; in the rise and fall of nations; in the life history of all things; and finally in the mental states of Man.

Beginning with the manifestations of Spirit – of THE ALL – it will be noticed that there is ever the Outpouring and the Indrawing; the "Outbreathing and Inbreathing of Brahm," as the Brahmans word it. Universes are created; reach their extreme low point of materiality; and then begin in their upward swing. Suns spring into being, and then their height of power being reached, the process of retrogression begins, and after aeons they become dead masses of matter, awaiting another impulse which starts again their inner energies into activity and a new solar life cycle is begun. And thus it is with all the worlds; they are born, grow and die; only to be reborn. And thus it is with all the things of shape and form; they swing from action to reaction; from birth to death; from activity to inactivity – and then back again. Thus it is with all living things; they are born, grow, and die – and then are reborn. So it is with all great movements, philosophies, creeds, fashions, governments, nations, and all else – birth, growth, maturity, decadence, death – and then new-birth. The swing of the pendulum is ever in evidence.

Night follows day; and day night. The pendulum swings from Summer to Winter, and then back again. The corpuscles, atoms, molecules, and all masses of matter, swing around the circle of their nature. There is no such thing as absolute rest, or cessation from movement, and all movement partakes of rhythm. The principle is of universal application. It may be applied to any question, or phenomena of any of the many planes of life. It may be applied to all phases of human activity. There is always the Rhythmic swing from one pole to the other. The Universal Pendulum is ever in motion. The Tides of Life flow in and out, according to Law.

The Principle of rhythm is well understood by modern science, and is considered a universal law as applied to material things. But the Hermetists carry the principle much further, and know that its manifestations and influence extend to the mental activities of Man, and that it accounts for the bewildering succession of moods, feelings and other annoying and perplexing changes that we notice in ourselves. But the Hermetists by studying the operations of this Principle have learned to escape some of its activities by Transmutation.

The Hermetic Masters long since discovered that while the Principle of Rhythm was invariable, and ever in evidence in mental phenomena, still there were two planes of its manifestation so far as mental phenomena are concerned. They discovered that there were two general planes of Consciousness, the Lower and the Higher, the understanding of which fact enabled them to rise to the higher plane and thus escape the swing of the Rhythmic pendulum which manifested on the lower plane. In other words, the swing of the pendulum occurred on the Unconscious Plane, and the Consciousness was not affected.

This they call the Law of Neutralization. Its operations consist in the raising of the Ego above the vibrations of the Unconscious Plane of mental activity, so that the negative-swing of the pendulum is not manifested in consciousness, and therefore they are not affected. It is akin to rising above a thing and letting it pass beneath you. The Hermetic Master, or advanced student, polarizes himself at the desired pole, and by a process akin to "refusing" to participate in the backward swing or, if you prefer, a "denial" of its influence over him, he stands firm in his polarized position, and allows the mental pendulum to swing back along the unconscious plane. All individuals who have attained any degree of self- mastery, accomplish this, more or less unknowingly, and by refusing to allow their moods and negative mental states to affect them, they apply the Law of Neutralization. The Master, however, carries this to a much higher degree of proficiency, and by the use of his Will he attains a degree of Poise and Mental Firmness almost impossible of belief on the part of those who allow themselves to be swung backward and forward by the mental pendulum of moods and feelings.

The importance of this will be appreciated by any thinking person who realizes what creatures of moods, feelings and emotion the majority of people are, and how little mastery of themselves they manifest. If you will stop and consider a moment, you will realize how much these swings of Rhythm have affected you in your life – how a period of Enthusiasm has been invariably followed by an opposite feeling and mood of Depression. Likewise, your moods and periods of Courage have been succeeded by equal moods of Fear. And so it has ever been with the majority of persons – tides of feeling have ever risen and fallen with them, but they have never suspected the cause or reason of the mental phenomena. An understanding of the workings of this Principle will give one the key to the Mastery of these rhythmic swings of feeling, and will enable him to know himself better and to avoid being carried away by these inflows and outflows. The Will is superior to the conscious manifestation of this Principle, although the Principle itself can never be destroyed. We may escape its effects, but the Principle operates, nevertheless. The pendulum ever swings, although we may escape being carried along with it.

There are other features of the operation of this Principle of Rhythm of which we wish to speak at this point. There comes into its operations that which is known as the Law of Compensation. One of the definitions or meanings of the word "Compensate" is, "to counterbalance" which is the sense in which the Hermetists use the term. It is this Law of Compensation to which the Kybalion refers when it says: "The measure of the swing to the right is the measure of the swing to the left; rhythm compensates."

The Law of Compensation is that the swing in one direction determines the swing in the opposite direction, or to the opposite pole – the one balances, or counterbalances, the other. On the Physical Plane we see many examples of this Law. The pendulum of the clock swings a certain distance to the right, and then an equal distance to the left. The seasons balance each other in the same way. The tides follow the same Law. And the same Law is manifested in all the phenomena of Rhythm. The pendulum, with a short swing in one direction, has but a short swing in the other; while the long swing to the right invariably means the long swing to the left. An object hurled upward to a certain height has an equal distance to traverse on its return. The force with which a projectile is sent upward a mile is reproduced when the projectile returns to the earth on its return journey. This Law is constant on the Physical Plane, as reference to the standard authorities will show you.

But the Hermetists carry it still further. They teach that a man's mental states are subject to the same Law. The man who enjoys keenly, is subject to keen suffering; while he who feels but little pain is capable of feeling but little joy. The pig suffers but little mentally, and enjoys but little – he is compensated. And on the other hand, there are other animals who enjoy keenly, but whose nervous organism and temperament cause them to suffer exquisite degrees of pain and so it is with Man. There are temperaments which permit of but low degrees of enjoyment, and equally low degrees of suffering; while there are others which permit the most intense enjoyment, but also the most intense suffering. The rule is that the capacity for pain and pleasure, in each individual, are balanced. The Law of Compensation is in full operation here.

But the Hermetists go still further in this matter. They teach that before one is able to enjoy a certain degree of pleasure, he must have swung as far, proportionately, toward the other pole of feeling. They hold, however, that the Negative is precedent to the Positive in this matter, that is to say that in experiencing a certain degree of pleasure it does not follow that he will have to "pay up for it" with a corresponding degree of pain; on the contrary, the pleasure is the Rhythmic swing, according to the Law of Compensation, for a degree of pain previously experienced either in the present life, or in a previous incarnation. This throws a new light on the Problem of Pain.

The Hermetists regard the chain of lives as continuous, and as forming a part of one life of the individual, so that in consequence the rhythmic swing is understood in this way, while it would be without meaning unless the truth of reincarnation is admitted.

But the Hermetists claim that the Master or advanced student is able, to a great degree, to escape the swing toward Pain, by the process of Neutralization before mentioned. By rising on to the higher plane of the Ego, much of the experience that comes to those dwelling on the lower plane is avoided and escaped.

The Law of Compensation plays an important part in the lives of men and women. It will be noticed that one generally "pays the price" of anything he possesses or lacks. If he has one thing, he lacks another – the balance is struck. No one can "keep his penny and have the bit of cake" at the same time. Everything has its pleasant and unpleasant sides. The things that one gains are always paid for by the things that one loses. The rich possess much that the poor lack, while the poor often possess things that are beyond the reach of the rich. The millionaire may have the inclination toward feasting, and the wealth wherewith to secure all the dainties and luxuries of the table, while he lacks the appetite to enjoy the same; he envies the appetite and digestion of the laborer who lacks the wealth and inclinations of the millionaire, and who gets more pleasure from his plain food than the millionaire could obtain even if his appetite were not jaded, nor his digestion ruined, for the wants, habits and inclinations differ. And so it is through life. The Law of Compensation is ever in operation, striving to balance and counter-balance, and always succeeding in time, even though several lives may be required for the return swing of the Pendulum of Rhythm.

CHAPTER XII

CAUSATION

"Every Cause has its Effect; every Effect has its Cause; everything happens according to Law; Chance is but a name for Law not recognized; there are many planes of causation, but nothing escapes the Law." – The Kybalion.

The great Sixth Hermetic Principle – the Principle of Cause and Effect – embodies the truth that Law pervades the Universe; that nothing happens by Chance; that Chance is merely a term indicating cause existing but not recognized or perceived; that phenomena is continuous, without break or exception.

The Principle of Cause and Effect underlies all scientific thought, ancient and modern, and was enunciated by the Hermetic Teachers in the earliest days. While many and varied disputes between the many schools of thought have since arisen, these disputes have been principally upon the details of the operations of the Principle, and still more often upon the meaning of certain words. The underlying Principle of Cause and Effect has been accepted as correct by practically all the thinkers of the world worthy of the name. To think otherwise would be to take the phenomena of the universe from the domain of Law and Order, and to relegate it to the control of the imaginary something which men have called "Chance."

A little consideration will show anyone that there is in reality no such thing as pure chance. Webster defines the word "Chance" as follows: "A supposed agent or mode of activity other than a force, law or purpose; the operation or activity of such agent; the supposed effect of such an agent; a happening; fortuity; casualty, etc." But a little consideration will show you that there can be no such agent as "Chance," in the sense of something outside of Law – something outside of Cause and Effect. How could there be a something acting in the phenomenal universe, independent of the laws, order, and continuity of the latter? Such a something would be entirely independent of the orderly trend of the universe, and therefore superior to it. We can imagine nothing outside of THE ALL being outside of the Law, and that only because THE ALL is the LAW in itself. There is no room in the universe for a something outside of and independent of Law. The existence of such a Something would render all Natural Laws ineffective, and would plunge the universe into chaotic disorder and lawlessness.

A careful examination will show that what we call "Chance" is merely an expression relating to obscure causes; causes that we cannot perceive; causes that we cannot understand. The word Chance is derived from a word Meaning "to fall" (as the falling of dice), the idea being that the fall of the dice (and many other happenings) are merely a "happening" unrelated to any cause. And this is the sense in which the term is generally employed. But when the matter is closely examined, it is seen that there is no chance whatsoever about the fall of the dice. Each time a die falls, and displays a certain number, it obeys a law as infallible as that which governs the revolution of the planets around the sun. Back of the fall of the die are causes, or chains of causes, running back further than the mind can follow. The position of the die in the box; the amount of muscular energy expended in the throw; the condition of the table, etc., etc., all are causes, the effect of which may be seen. But back of these seen causes there are chains of unseen preceding causes, all of which had a bearing upon the number of the die which fell uppermost.

If a die be cast a great number of times, it will be found that the numbers shown will be about equal, that is, there will be an equal number of one-spot, two-spot, etc., coming uppermost. Toss a penny in the air, and it may come down either "heads" or "tails"; but make a sufficient number of tosses, and the heads and tails will about even up. This is the operation of the law of average. But both the average and the single toss come under the Law of Cause and Effect, and if we were able to examine into the preceding causes, it would be clearly seen that it was simply impossible for the die to fall other than it did, under the same circumstances and at the same time. Given the same causes, the same results will follow. There is always a "cause" and a "because" to every event. Nothing ever "happens" without a cause, or rather a chain of causes.

Some confusion has arisen in the minds of persons considering this Principle, from the fact that they were unable to explain how one thing could cause another thing – that is, be the "creator" of the second thing. As a matter of fact, no "thing" ever causes or "creates" another "thing." Cause and Effect deals merely with "events." An "event" is "that which comes, arrives or happens, as a result or consequent of some preceding event." No event "creates" another event, but is merely a preceding link in the great orderly chain of events flowing from the creative energy of THE ALL. There is a continuity between all events precedent, consequent and subsequent. There is a relation existing between everything that has gone before, and everything that follows. A stone is dislodged from a mountain side and crashes through a roof of a cottage in the valley below. At first sight we regard this as a chance effect, but when we examine the matter we find a great chain of causes behind it. In the first place there was the rain which softened the earth supporting the stone and which allowed it to fall; then back of that was the influence of the sun, other rains, etc., which gradually disintegrated the piece of rock from a larger piece; then there were the causes which led to the formation of the mountain, and its upheaval by convulsions of nature, and so on *ad infinitum.* Then we might follow up the causes behind the rain, etc. Then we might consider the existence of the roof. In short, we would soon find ourselves involved in a mesh of cause and effect, from which we would soon strive to extricate ourselves.

Just as a man has two parents, and four grandparents, and eight great-grandparents, and sixteen great-great-grandparents, and so on until when, say, forty generations are calculated the numbers of ancestors run into many millions – so it is with the number of causes behind even the most trifling event or phenomena, such as the passage of a tiny speck of soot before your eye. It is not an easy matter to trace the bit of soot back to the early period of the world's history when it formed a part of a massive tree-trunk, which was afterward converted into coal, and so on, until as the speck of soot it now passes before your vision on its way to other adventures. And a mighty chain of events, causes and effects, brought it to its present condition, and the latter is but one of the chain of events which will go to produce other events hundreds of years from now. One of the series of events arising from the tiny bit of soot was the writing of these lines, which caused the typesetter to perform certain work; the proof-reader to do likewise; and which will arouse certain thoughts in your mind, and that of others, which in turn will affect others, and so on, and on, and on, beyond the ability of man to think further – and all from the passage of a tiny bit of soot, all of which shows the relativity and association of things, and the further fact that "there is no great; there is no small, in the mind that causeth all."

Stop to think a moment. If a certain man had not met a certain maid, away back in the dim period of the Stone Age – you who are now reading these lines would not now be here. And if, perhaps, the same couple had failed to meet, we who now write these lines would not now be here. And the very act of writing, on our part, and the act of reading, on yours, will affect not only the respective lives of yourself and ourselves, but will also have a direct, or indirect, affect upon many other people now living and who will live in the ages to come. Every thought we think, every act we perform, has its direct and indirect results which fit into the great chain of Cause and Effect.

We do not wish to enter into a consideration of Free Will, or Determinism, in this work, for various reasons. Among the many reasons, is the principal one that neither side of the controversy is entirely right – in fact, both sides are partially right, according to the Hermetic Teachings. The Principle of Polarity shows that both are but Half-Truths the opposing poles of Truth. The Teachings are that a man may be both Free and yet bound by Necessity, depending upon the meaning of the terms, and the height of Truth from which the matter is examined. The ancient writers express the matter thus: "The further the creation is from the Centre, the more it is bound; the nearer the Centre it reaches, the nearer Free is it."

The majority of people are more or less the slaves of heredity, environment, etc., and manifest very little Freedom. They are swayed by the opinions, customs and thoughts of the outside world, and also by their emotions, feelings, moods, etc. They manifest no Mastery, worthy of the name. They indignantly repudiate this assertion, saying, "Why, I certainly am free to act and do as I please – I do just what I want to do," but they fail to explain whence arise the "want to" and "as I please." What makes them "want to" do one thing in preference to another; what makes them "please" to do this, and not do that? Is there no "because" to their "pleasing" and "Wanting"? The Master can change these "pleases" and "wants" into others at the opposite end of the mental pole. He is able to "Will to will," instead of to will because some feeling, mood, emotion, or environmental suggestion arouses a tendency or desire within him so to do.

The majority of people are carried along like the falling stone, obedient to environment, outside influences and internal moods, desires, etc., not to speak of the desires and wills of others stronger than themselves, heredity, environment, and suggestion, carrying them along without resistance on their part, or the exercise of the Will. Moved like the pawns on the checkerboard of life, they play their parts and are laid aside after the game is over. But the Masters, knowing the rules of the game, rise above the plane of material life, and placing themselves in touch with the higher powers of their nature, dominate their own moods, characters, qualities, and polarity, as well as the environment surrounding them and thus become Movers in the game, instead of Pawns – Causes instead of Effects. The Masters do not escape the Causation of the higher planes, but fall in with the higher laws, and thus master circumstances on the lower plane. They thus form a conscious part of the Law, instead of being mere blind instruments. While they Serve on the Higher Planes, they Rule on the Material Plane.

But, on higher and on lower, the Law is always in operation. There is no such thing as Chance. The blind goddess has been abolished by Reason. We are able to see now, with eyes made clear by knowledge, that everything is governed by Universal Law – that the infinite number of laws are but manifestations of the One Great Law – the LAW which is THE ALL. It is true indeed that not a sparrow drops unnoticed by the Mind of THE ALL – that even the hairs on our head are numbered – as the scriptures have said. There is nothing outside of Law; nothing that happens contrary to it. And yet, do not make the mistake of supposing that Man is but a blind automaton – far from that. The Hermetic Teachings are that Man may use Law to overcome laws, and that the higher will always prevail against the lower, until at last he has reached the stage in which he seeks refuge in the LAW itself, and laughs the phenomenal laws to scorn. Are you able to grasp the inner meaning of this?

CHAPTER XIII

GENDER

"Gender is in everything; everything has its Masculine and Feminine Principles; Gender manifests on all planes." – The Kybalion.

The great Seventh Hermetic Principle – the Principle of Gender – embodies the truth that there is Gender manifested in everything – that the Masculine and Feminine principles are ever present and active in all phases of phenomena, on each and every plane of life. At this point we think it well to call your attention to the fact that Gender, in its Hermetic sense, and Sex in the ordinarily accepted use of the term, are not the same.

The word "Gender" is derived from the Latin root meaning "to beget; to procreate; to generate; to create; to produce." A moment's consideration will show you that the word has a much broader and more general meaning than the term "Sex," the latter referring to the physical distinctions between male and female living things. Sex is merely a manifestation of Gender on a certain plane of the Great Physical Plane – the plane of organic life. We wish to impress this distinction upon your minds, for the reason that certain writers, who have acquired a smattering of the Hermetic Philosophy, have sought to identify this Seventh Hermetic Principle with wild and fanciful, and often reprehensible, theories and teachings regarding Sex.

The office of Gender is solely that of creating, producing, generating, etc., and its manifestations are visible on every plane of phenomena. It is somewhat difficult to produce proofs of this along scientific lines, for the reason that science has not as yet recognized this Principle as of universal application. But still some proofs are forthcoming from scientific sources. In the first place, we find a distinct manifestation of the Principle of Gender among the corpuscles, ions, or electrons, which constitute the basis of Matter as science now knows the latter, and which by forming certain combinations form the Atom, which until lately was regarded as final and indivisible.

The latest word of science is that the atom is composed of a multitude of corpuscles, electrons, or ions (the various names being applied by different authorities) revolving around each other and vibrating at a high degree and intensity. But the accompanying statement is made that the formation of the atom is really due to the clustering of negative corpuscles around a positive one – the positive corpuscles seeming to exert a certain influence upon the negative corpuscles, causing the latter to assume certain combinations and thus "create" or "generate" an atom. This is in line with the most ancient Hermetic Teachings, which have always identified the Masculine principle of Gender with the "Positive," and the Feminine with the "Negative" Poles of Electricity (so called).

Now a word at this point regarding this identification. The public mind has formed an entirely erroneous impression regarding the qualities of the so-called "Negative" pole of electrified or magnetized Matter. The terms Positive and Negative are very wrongly applied to this phenomenon by science. The word Positive means something real and strong, as compared with a Negative unreality or weakness. Nothing is further from the real facts of electrical phenomenon. The so-called Negative pole of the battery is really the pole in and by which the generation or production of new forms and energies is manifested. There is nothing "negative" about it. The best scientific authorities now use the word "Cathode" in place of "Negative," the word Cathode coming from the Greek root meaning "descent; the path of generation, etc," From the Cathode pole emerge the swarm of electrons or corpuscles; from the same pole emerge those wonderful "rays" which have revolutionized scientific conceptions during the past decade. The Cathode pole is the Mother of all of the strange phenomena which have rendered useless the old textbooks, and which have caused many long accepted theories to be relegated to the scrap-pile of scientific speculation. The Cathode, or Negative Pole, is the Mother Principle of Electrical Phenomena, and of the finest forms of matter as yet known to science. So you see we are justified in refusing to use the term "Negative" in our consideration of the subject, and in insisting upon substituting the word "Feminine" for the old term. The facts of the case bear us out in this, without taking the Hermetic Teachings into consideration. And so we shall use the word "Feminine" in the place of "Negative" in speaking of that pole of activity.

The latest scientific teachings are that the creative corpuscles or electrons are Feminine (science says "they are composed of negative electricity" – we say they are composed of Feminine energy). A Feminine corpuscle becomes detached from, or rather leaves, a Masculine corpuscle, and starts on a new career. It actively seeks a union with a Masculine corpuscle, being urged thereto by the natural impulse to create new forms of Matter or Energy. One writer goes so far as to use the term "it at once seeks, of its own volition, a union," etc. This detachment and uniting form the basis of the greater part of the activities of the chemical world. When the Feminine corpuscle unites with a Masculine corpuscle, a certain process is begun. The Feminine particles vibrate rapidly under the influence of the Masculine energy, and circle rapidly around the latter. The result is the birth of a new atom. This new atom is really composed of a union of the Masculine and Feminine electrons, or corpuscles, but when the union is formed the atom is a separate thing, having certain properties, but no longer manifesting the property of free electricity. The process of detachment or separation of the Feminine electrons is called "ionization." These electrons, or corpuscles, are the most active workers in Nature's field. Arising from their unions, or combinations, manifest the varied phenomena of light, heat, electricity, magnetism, attraction, repulsion, chemical affinity and the reverse, and similar phenomena. And all this arises from the operation of the Principle of Gender on the plane of Energy.

The part of the Masculine principle seems to be that of directing a certain inherent energy toward the Feminine principle, and thus starting into activity the creative processes. But the Feminine principle is the one always doing the active creative work – and this is so on all planes. And yet, each principle is incapable of operative energy without the assistance of the other. In some of the forms of life, the two principles are combined in one organism. For that matter, everything in the organic world manifests both genders – there is always the Masculine present in the Feminine form, and the Feminine form. The Hermetic Teachings include much regarding the operation of the two principles of Gender in the production and manifestation of various forms of energy, etc., but we do not deem it expedient to go into detail regarding the same at this point, because we are unable to back up the same with scientific proof, for the reason that science has not as yet progressed thus far. But the example we have given you of the phenomena of the electrons or corpuscles will show you that science is on the right path, and will also give you a general idea of the underlying principles.

Some leading scientific investigators have announced their belief that in the formation of crystals there was to be found something that corresponded to "sex-activity" which is another straw showing the direction the scientific winds are blowing. And each year will bring other facts to corroborate the correctness of the Hermetic Principle of Gender. It will be found that Gender is in constant operation and manifestation in the field of inorganic matter, and in the field of Energy or Force. Electricity is now generally regarded as the "Something" into which all other forms of energy seem to melt or dissolve. The "Electrical Theory of the Universe" is the latest scientific doctrine, and is growing rapidly in popularity and general acceptance. And it thus follows that if we are able to discover in the phenomena of electricity – even at the very root and source of its manifestations a clear and unmistakable evidence of the presence of Gender and its activities, we are justified in asking you to believe that science at last has offered proofs of the existence in all universal phenomena of that great Hermetic Principle – the Principle of Gender.

It is not necessary to take up your time with the well known phenomena of the "attraction and repulsion" of the atoms; chemical affinity; the "loves and hates" of the atomic particles; the attraction or cohesion between the molecules of matter. These facts are too well known to need extended comment from us. But, have you ever considered that all of these things are manifestations of the Gender Principle? Can you not see that the phenomena is "on all fours" with that of the corpuscles or electrons? And more than this, can you not see the reasonableness of the Hermetic Teachings which assert that the very Law of Gravitation – that strange attraction by reason of which all particles and bodies of matter in the universe tend toward each other is but another manifestation of the Principle of Gender, which operates in the direction of attracting the Masculine to the Feminine energies, and vice versa? We cannot offer you scientific proof of this at this time – but examine the phenomena in the light of the Hermetic Teachings on the subject, and see if you have not a better working hypothesis than any offered by physical science. Submit all physical phenomena to the test, and you will discern the Principle of Gender ever in evidence.

Let us now pass on to a consideration of the operation of the Principle on the Mental Plane. Many interesting features are there awaiting examination.

CHAPTER XIV

MENTAL GENDER

Students of psychology who have followed the modern trend of thought along the lines of mental phenomena are struck by the persistence of the dual-mind idea which has manifested itself so strongly during the past ten or fifteen years, and which has given rise to a number of plausible theories regarding the nature and constitution of these "two minds." The late Thomson J. Hudson attained great popularity in 1893 by advancing his well-known theory of the "objective and subjective minds" which he held existed in every individual. Other writers have attracted almost equal attention by the theories regarding the "conscious and subconscious minds"; the "voluntary and involuntary minds"; "the active and passive minds," etc., etc. The theories of the various writers differ from each other, but there remains the underlying principle of "the duality of mind."

The student of the Hermetic Philosophy is tempted to smile when he reads and hears of these many "new theories" regarding the duality of mind, each school adhering tenaciously to its own pet theories, and each claiming to have "discovered the truth." The student turns back the pages of occult history, and away back in the dim beginnings of occult teachings he finds references to the ancient Hermetic doctrine of the Principle of Gender on the Mental Plane – the manifestation of Mental Gender. And examining further he finds that the ancient philosophy took cognizance of the phenomenon of the "dual mind," and accounted for it by the theory of Mental Gender. This idea of Mental Gender may be explained in a few words to students who are familiar with the modern theories just alluded to.

The Masculine Principle of Mind corresponds to the so-called Objective Mind; Conscious Mind; Voluntary Mind; Active Mind, etc. And the Feminine Principle of Mind corresponds to the so-called Subjective Mind; Sub-conscious Mind; Involuntary Mind; Passive Mind, etc. Of course the Hermetic Teachings do not agree with the many modern theories regarding the nature of the two phases of mind, nor does it admit many of the facts claimed for the two respective aspects – some of the said theories and claims being very far-fetched and incapable of standing the test of experiment and demonstration. We point to the phases of agreement merely for the purpose of helping the student to assimilate his previously acquired knowledge with the teachings of the Hermetic Philosophy. Students of Hudson will notice the statement at the beginning of his second chapter of "The Law of Psychic Phenomena," that: "The mystic jargon of the Hermetic philosophers discloses the same general idea" i.e., the duality of mind. If Dr. Hudson had taken the time and trouble to decipher a little of "the mystic jargon of the Hermetic Philosophy," he might have received much light upon the subject of "the dual mind" – but then, perhaps, his most interesting work might not have been written. Let us now consider the Hermetic Teachings regarding Mental Gender.

The Hermetic Teachers impart their instruction regarding this subject by bidding their students examine the report of their consciousness regarding their Self. The students are bidden to turn their attention inward upon the Self dwelling within each. Each student is led to see that his consciousness gives him first a report of the existence of his Self – the report is "I Am." This at first seems to be the final words from the consciousness, but a little further examination discloses the fact that this "I Am" may be separated or split into two distinct parts, or aspects, which while working in unison and in conjunction, yet, nevertheless, may be separated in consciousness.

While at first there seems to be only an "I" existing, a more careful and closer examination reveals the fact that there exists an "I" and a "Me." These mental twins differ in their characteristics and nature, and an examination of their nature and the phenomena arising from the same will throw much light upon many of the problems of mental influence.

Let us begin with a consideration of the Me, which is usually mistaken for the I by the student, until he presses the inquiry a little further back into the recesses of consciousness. A man thinks of his Self (in its aspect of Me) as being composed of certain feelings, tastes likes, dislikes, habits, peculiar ties, characteristics, etc., all of which go to make up his personality, or the "Self" known to himself and others. He knows that these emotions and feelings change; are born and die away; are subject to the Principle of Rhythm, and the Principle of Polarity, which take him from one extreme of feeling to another. He also thinks of the "Me" as being certain knowledge gathered together in his mind, and thus forming a part of himself. This is the "Me" of a man.

But we have proceeded too hastily. The "Me" of many men may be said to consist largely of their consciousness of the body and their physical appetites, etc. Their consciousness being largely bound up with their bodily nature, they practically "live there." Some men even go so far as to regard their personal apparel as a part of their "Me" and actually seem to consider it a part of themselves. A writer has humorously said that "men consist of three parts – soul, body and clothes." These "clothes conscious" people would lose their personality if divested of their clothing by savages upon the occasion of a shipwreck. But even many who are not so closely bound up with the idea of personal raiment stick closely to the consciousness of their bodies being their "Me" They cannot conceive of a Self independent of the body. Their mind seems to them to be practically "a something belonging to" their body – which in many cases it is indeed.

But as man rises in the scale of consciousness he is able to disentangle his "Me" from his idea of body, and is able to think of his body as "belonging to" the mental part of him. But even then he is very apt to identify the "Me" entirely with the mental states, feelings, etc., which he feels to exist within him. He is very apt to consider these internal states as identical with himself, instead of their being simply "things" produced by some part of his mentality, and existing within him – of him, and in him, but still not "himself." He sees that he may change these internal states of feelings by all effort of will, and that he may produce a feeling or state of an exactly opposite nature, in the same way, and yet the same "Me" exists. And so after a while he is able to set aside these various mental states, emotions, feelings, habits, qualities, characteristics, and other personal mental belongings – he is able to set them aside in the "not-me" collection of curiosities and encumbrances, as well as valuable possessions. This requires much mental concentration and power of mental analysis on the part of the student. But still the task is possible for the advanced student, and even those not so far advanced are able to see, in the imagination, how the process may be performed.

After this laying-aside process has been performed, the student will find himself in conscious possession of a "Self" which may be considered in its "I" and "Me" dual aspects. The "Me" will be felt to be a Something mental in which thoughts, ideas, emotions, feelings, and other mental states may be produced. It may be considered as the "mental womb," as the ancients styled it – capable of generating mental offspring. It reports to the consciousness as a "Me" with latent powers of creation and generation of mental progeny of all sorts and kinds. Its powers of creative energy are felt to be enormous. But still it seems to be conscious that it must receive some form of energy from either its "I" companion, or else from some other "I" ere it is able to bring into being its mental creations. This consciousness brings with it a realization of an enormous capacity for mental work and creative ability.

But the student soon finds that this is not all that he finds within his inner consciousness. He finds that there exists a mental Something which is able to Will that the "Me" act along certain creative lines, and which is also able to stand aside and witness the mental creation. This part of himself he is taught to call his "I." He is able to rest in its consciousness at will. He finds there not a consciousness of an ability to generate and actively create, in the sense of the gradual process attendant upon mental operations, but rather a sense and consciousness of an ability to project an energy from the "I" to the "Me" – a process of "willing" that the mental creation begin and proceed. He also finds that the "I" is able to stand aside and witness the operations of the "Me's" mental creation and generation. There is this dual aspect in the mind of every person. The "I" represents the Masculine Principle of Mental Gender – the "Me" represents the Female Principle. The "I" represents the Aspect of Being; the "Me" the Aspect of Becoming. You will notice that the Principle of Correspondence operates on this plane just as it does upon the great plane upon which the creation of Universes is performed. The two are similar in kind, although vastly different in degree. "As above, so below; as below, so above."

These aspects of mind – the Masculine and Feminine Principles – the "I" and the "Me" – considered in connection with the well-known mental and psychic phenomena, give the master-key to these dimly known regions of mental operation and manifestation. The principle of Mental Gender gives the truth underlying the whole field of the phenomena of mental influence, etc.

The tendency of the Feminine Principle is always in the direction of receiving impressions, while the tendency of the Masculine Principle is always in the direction of giving out, or expressing. The Feminine Principle has much more varied field of operation than has the Masculine Principle. The Feminine Principle conducts the work of generating new thoughts, concepts, ideas, including the work of the imagination. The Masculine Principle contents itself with the work of the "Will" in its varied phases. And yet, without the active aid of the Will of the Masculine Principle, the Feminine Principle is apt to rest content with generating mental images which are the result of impressions received from outside, instead of producing original mental creations.

Persons who can give continued attention and thought to a subject actively employ both of the Mental Principles – the Feminine in the work of the mental generation, and the Masculine Will in stimulating and energizing the creative portion of the mind. The majority of persons really employ the Masculine Principle but little, and are content to live according to the thoughts and ideas instilled into the "Me" from the "I" of other minds. But it is not our purpose to dwell upon this phase of the subject, which may be studied from any good text-book upon psychology, with the key that we have given you regarding Mental Gender.

The student of Psychic Phenomena is aware of the wonderful phenomena classified under the head of Telepathy; Thought Transference; Mental Influence; Suggestion; Hypnotism, etc. Many have sought for an explanation of these varied phases of phenomena under the theories of the various "dual mind" teachers. And in a measure they are right, for there is clearly a manifestation of two distinct phases of mental activity. But if such students will consider these "dual minds" in the light of the Hermetic Teachings regarding Vibrations and Mental Gender, they will see that the long sought for key is at hand.

In the phenomena of Telepathy it is seen how the Vibratory Energy of the Masculine Principle is projected toward the Feminine Principle of another person, and the latter takes the seed-thought and allows it to develop into maturity. In the same way Suggestion and Hypnotism operates. The Masculine Principle of the person giving the suggestions directs a stream of Vibratory Energy or Will-Power toward the Feminine Principle of the other person, and the latter accepting it makes it its own and acts and thinks accordingly. An idea thus lodged in the mind of another person grows and develops, and in time is regarded as the rightful mental offspring of the individual, whereas it is in reality like the cuckoo egg placed in the sparrows nest, where it destroys the rightful offspring and makes itself at home. The normal method is for the Masculine and Feminine Principles in a person's mind to co-ordinate and act harmoniously in conjunction with each other, but, unfortunately, the Masculine Principle in the average person is too lazy to act – the display of Will-Power is too slight – and the consequence is that such persons are ruled almost entirely by the minds and wills of other persons, whom they allow to do their thinking and willing for them. How few original thoughts or original actions are performed by the average person? Are not the majority of persons mere shadows and echoes of others having stronger wills or minds than themselves? The trouble is that the average person dwells almost altogether in his "Me" consciousness and does not realize that he has such a thing as an "I." He is polarized in his Feminine Principle of Mind, and the Masculine Principle, in which is lodged the Will, is allowed to remain inactive and not employed.

The strong men and women of the world invariably manifest the Masculine Principle of Will, and their strength depends materially upon this fact. Instead of living upon the impressions made upon their minds by others, they dominate their own minds by their Will, obtaining the kind of mental images desired, and moreover dominate the minds of others likewise, in the same manner. Look at the strong people, how they manage to implant their seed-thoughts in the minds of the masses of the people, thus causing the latter to think thoughts in accordance with the desires and wills of the strong individuals. This is why the masses of people are such sheeplike creatures, never originating an idea of their own, nor using their own powers of mental activity.

The manifestation of Mental Gender may be noticed all around us in everyday life. The magnetic persons are those who are able to use the Masculine Principle in the way of impressing their ideas upon others. The actor who makes people weep or cry as he wills, is employing this principle. And so is the successful orator, statesman, preacher, writer or other people who are before the public attention. The peculiar influence exerted by some people over others is due to the manifestation of Mental Gender, along the Vibrational lines above indicated. In this principle lies the secret of personal magnetism, personal influence, fascination, etc., as well as the phenomena generally grouped under the name of Hypnotism.

The student who has familiarized himself with the phenomena generally spoken of as "psychic" will have discovered the important part played in the said phenomena by that force which science has styled "Suggestion," by which term is meant the process or method whereby an idea is transferred to, or "impressed upon" the mind of another, causing the second mind to act in accordance therewith. A correct understanding of Suggestion is necessary in order to intelligently comprehend the varied psychical phenomena which Suggestion underlies. But, still more is a knowledge of Vibration and Mental Gender necessary for the student of Suggestion. For the whole principle of Suggestion depends upon the principle of Mental Gender and Vibration.

It is customary for the writers and teachers of Suggestion to explain that it is the "objective or voluntary" mind which make the mental impression, or suggestion, upon the "subjective or involuntary" mind. But they do not describe the process or give us any analogy in nature whereby we may more readily comprehend the idea. But if you will think of the matter in the light of the Hermetic Teachings you will be able to see that the energizing of the Feminine Principle by the Vibratory Energy of the Masculine Principle is in accordance to the universal laws of nature, and that the natural world affords countless analogies whereby the principle may be understood. In fact, the Hermetic Teachings show that the very creation of the Universe follows the same law, and that in all creative manifestations, upon the planes of the spiritual, the mental, and the physical, there is always in operation this principle of Gender – this manifestation of the Masculine and the Feminine Principles. "As above, so below; as below, so above." And more than this, when the principle of Mental Gender is once grasped and understood, the varied phenomena of psychology at once becomes capable of intelligent classification and study, instead of being very much in the dark. The principle "works out" in practice, because it is based upon the immutable universal laws of life.

We shall not enter into an extended discussion of, or description of, the varied phenomena of mental influence or psychic activity. There are many books, many of them quite good, which have been written and published on this subject of late years. The main facts stated in these various books are correct, although the several writers have attempted to explain the phenomena by various pet theories of their own. The student may acquaint himself with these matters, and by using the theory of Mental Gender he will be able to bring order out of the chaos of conflicting theory and teachings, and may, moreover, readily make himself a master of the subject if he be so inclined. The purpose of this work is not to give an extended account of psychic phenomena but rather to give to the student a master-key whereby He may unlock the many doors leading into the parts of the Temple of Knowledge which he may wish to explore. We feel that in this consideration of the teachings of The Kybalion, one may find an explanation which will serve to clear away many perplexing difficulties – a key that will unlock many doors. What is the use of going into detail regarding all of the many features of psychic phenomena and mental science, provided we place in the hands of the student the means whereby he may acquaint himself fully regarding any phase of the subject which may interest him. With the aid of The Kybalion one may go through any occult library anew, the old Light from Egypt illuminating many dark pages, and obscure subjects. That is the purpose of this book. We do not come expounding a new philosophy, but rather furnishing the outlines of a great world-old teaching which will make clear the teachings of others – which will serve as a Great Reconciler of differing theories, and opposing doctrines.

CHAPTER XV

HERMETIC AXIOMS

"The possession of Knowledge, unless accompanied by a manifestation and expression in Action, is like the hoarding of precious metals – a vain and foolish thing. Knowledge, like wealth, is intended for Use. The Law of Use is Universal, and he who violates it suffers by reason of his conflict with natural forces."
– The Kybalion.

The Hermetic Teachings, while always having been kept securely locked up in the minds of the fortunate possessors thereof, for reasons which we have already stated, were never intended to be merely stored away and secreted. The Law of Use is dwelt upon in the Teachings, as you may see by reference to the above quotation from The Kybalion, which states it forcibly. Knowledge without Use and Expression is a vain thing, bringing no good to its possessor, or to the race. Beware of Mental Miserliness, and express into Action that which you have learned. Study the Axioms and Aphorisms, but practice them also.

We give below some of the more important Hermetic Axioms, from The Kybalion, with a few comments added to each. Make these your own, and practice and use them, for they are not really your own until you have Used them.

"To change your mood or mental state – change your vibration."
– The Kybalion.

One may change his mental vibrations by an effort of Will, in the direction of deliberately fixing the Attention upon a more desirable state. Will directs the Attention, and Attention changes the Vibration. Cultivate the Art of Attention, by means of the Will, and you have solved the secret of the Mastery of Moods and Mental States.

"To destroy an undesirable rate of mental vibration, put into operation the principle of Polarity and concentrate upon the opposite pole to that which you desire to suppress. Kill out the undesirable by changing its polarity."
– The Kybalion.

This is one of the most important of the Hermetic Formulas. It is based upon true scientific principles. We have shown you that a mental state and its opposite were merely the two poles of one thing, and that by Mental Transmutation the polarity might be reversed. This Principle is known to modern psychologists, who apply it to the breaking up of undesirable habits by bidding their students concentrate upon the opposite quality. If you are possessed of Fear, do not waste time trying to "kill out" Fear, but instead cultivate the quality of Courage, and the Fear will disappear. Some writers have expressed this idea most forcibly by using the illustration of the dark room. You do not have to shovel out or sweep out the Darkness, but by merely opening the shutters and letting in the Light the Darkness has disappeared. To kill out a Negative quality, concentrate upon the Positive Pole of that same quality, and the vibrations will gradually change from Negative to Positive, until finally you will become polarized on the Positive pole instead of the Negative. The reverse is also true, as many have found out to their sorrow, when they have allowed themselves to vibrate too constantly on the Negative pole of things. By changing your polarity you may master your moods, change your mental states, remake your disposition, and build up character. Much of the Mental Mastery of the advanced Hermetics is due to this application of Polarity, which is one of the important aspects of Mental Transmutation. Remember the Hermetic Axiom (quoted previously), which says:

"Mind (as well as metals and elements) may be transmuted from state to state; degree to degree, condition to condition; pole to pole; vibration to vibration."
– The Kybalion.

The mastery of Polarization is the mastery of the fundamental principles of Mental Transmutation or Mental Alchemy, for unless one acquires the art of changing his own polarity, he will be unable to affect his environment. An understanding of this principle will enable one to change his own Polarity, as well as that of others, if he will but devote the time, care, study and practice necessary to master the art. The principle is true, but the results obtained depend upon the persistent patience and practice of the student.

"Rhythm may be neutralized by an application of the Art of Polarization."
– The Kybalion.

As we have explained in previous chapters, the Hermetists hold that the Principle of Rhythm manifests on the Mental Plane as well as on the Physical Plane, and that the bewildering succession of moods, feelings, emotions, and other mental states, are due to the backward and forward swing of the mental pendulum, which carries us from one extreme of feeling to the other. The Hermetists also teach that the Law of Neutralization enables one, to a great extent, to overcome the operation of Rhythm in consciousness. As we have explained, there is a Higher Plane of Consciousness, as well as the ordinary Lower Plane, and the Master by rising mentally to the Higher Plane causes the swing of the mental pendulum to manifest on the Lower Plane, and he, dwelling on his Higher Plane, escapes the consciousness of the swing backward. This is effected by polarizing on the Higher Self, and thus raising the mental vibrations of the Ego above those of the ordinary plane of consciousness. It is akin to rising above a thing and allowing it to pass beneath you. The advanced Hermetist polarizes himself at the Positive Pole of his Being – the "I Am" pole rather than the pole of personality and by "refusing" and "denying" the operation of Rhythm, raises himself above its plane of consciousness, and standing firm in his Statement of Being he allows the pendulum to swing back on the Lower Plane without changing his Polarity. This is accomplished by all individuals who have attained any degree of self-mastery, whether they understand the law or not. Such persons simply "refuse" to allow themselves to be swung back by the pendulum of mood and emotion, and by steadfastly affirming the superiority they remain polarized on the Positive pole. The Master, of course, attains a far greater degree of proficiency, because he understands the law which he is overcoming by a higher law, and by the use of his Will he attains a degree of Poise and Mental Steadfastness almost impossible of belief on the part of those who allow themselves to be swung backward and forward by the mental pendulum of moods and feelings.

Remember always, however, that you do not really destroy the Principle of Rhythm, for that is indestructible. You simply overcome one law by counter-balancing it with another and thus maintain an equilibrium. The laws of balance and counter-balance are in operation on the mental as well as on the physical planes, and an understanding of these laws enables one to seem to overthrow laws, whereas he is merely exerting a counterbalance.

"Nothing escapes the Principle of Cause and Effect, but there are many Planes of Causation, and one may use the laws of the higher to overcome the laws of the lower." – The Kybalion.

By an understanding of the practice of Polarization, the Hermetists rise to a higher plane of Causation and thus counter-balance the laws of the lower planes of Causation. By rising above the plane of ordinary Causes they become themselves, in a degree, Causes instead of being merely Caused. By being able to master their own moods and feelings, and by being able to neutralize Rhythm, as we have already explained, they are able to escape a great part of the operations of Cause and Effect on the ordinary plane. The masses of people are carried along, obedient to their environment; the wills and desires of others stronger than themselves; the effects of inherited tendencies; the suggestions of those about them; and other outward causes; which tend to move them about on the chess-board of life like mere pawns. By rising above these influencing causes, the advanced Hermetists seek a higher plane of mental action, and by dominating their moods, emotions, impulses and feelings, they create for themselves new characters, qualities and powers, by which they overcome their ordinary environment, and thus become practically Players instead of mere Pawns. Such people help to play the game of life understandingly, instead of being moved about this way and that way by stronger influences and powers and wills. They use the Principle of Cause and Effect, instead of being used by it. Of course, even the highest are subject to the Principle as it manifests on the higher planes, but on the lower planes of activity, they are Masters instead of Slaves. As The Kybalion says:

"The wise ones serve on the higher, but rule on the lower. They obey the laws coming from above them, But on their own plane, and those below them they rule and give orders. And, yet, in so doing, they form a part of the Principle, instead of opposing it. The wise man falls in with the Law, and by understanding its movements he operates it instead of being its blind slave. Just as does the skilled swimmer turn this way and that way, going and coming as he will, instead of being as the log which is carried here and there – so is the wise man as compared to the ordinary man – and yet both swimmer and log; wise man and fool, are subject to Law. He who understands this is well on the road to Mastery."

– The Kybalion.

In conclusion let us again call your attention to the Hermetic Axiom:

"True Hermetic Transmutation is a Mental Art." – The Kybalion.

In the above axiom, the Hermetists teach that the great work of influencing one's environment is accomplished by Mental Power. The Universe being wholly mental, it follows that it may be ruled only by Mentality. And in this truth is to be found an explanation of all the phenomena and manifestations of the various mental powers which are attracting so much attention and study in these earlier years of the Twentieth Century. Back of and under the teachings of the various cults and schools, remains ever constant the Principle of the Mental Substance of the Universe. If the Universe be Mental in its substantial nature, then it follows that Mental Transmutation must change the conditions and phenomena of the Universe. If the Universe is Mental, then Mind must be the highest power affecting its phenomena. If this be understood then all the so-called "miracles" and "wonder-workings" are seen plainly for what they are.

"THE ALL is MIND; The Universe is Mental."

The Kybalion.

finis

This ancient tablet was the first revelation of God to man. While its mystery is practically unknown to this age, it may also be one of the earliest representations of the Hiramic Legend.

HERE BEGINS

THE
EMERALD TABLET
OF HERMES

HISTORY OF THE TABLET

The Tablet probably first appeared in the West in editions of the psuedo-Aristotlean *Secretum Secretorum* which was actually a translation of the *Kitab Sirr al-Asar*, a book of advice to kings which was translated into latin by Johannes Hispalensis c. 1140, and by Philip of Tripoli c.1243. Other translations of the Tablet may have been made during the same period by Plato of Tivoli and Hugh of Santalla, perhaps from different sources.

The date of the *Kitab Sirr al-Asar* is uncertain, though c.800 has been suggested and it is not clear when the tablet became part of this work.

Holmyard was the first to find another early arabic version (Ruska found a 12th century recension claiming to have been dictated by Sergius of Nablus) in the *Kitab Ustuqus al-Uss al-Thani* (Second Book of the Elements of Foundation) attributed to Jabir. Shortly after Ruska found another version appended to the *Kitab Sirr al-Khaliqa wa San`at al-Tabi`a* (Book of the Secret of Creation and the Art of Nature), which is also known as the *Kitab Balaniyus al-Hakim fi'l-`Ilal* (book of Balinas the wise on the Causes). It has been proposed that this book was written/may have been written as early as 650, and was definitely finished by the Caliphate of al-Ma'mun (813-33).

Scholars have seen similarities between this book and the Syriac *Book of Treasures* written by Job of Odessa (9th century) and more interestingly the Greek writings of the bishop Nemesius of Emesa in Syria from the mid fourth century. However though this suggests a possible Syriac source, none of these writings contain the tablet.

Balinas is usually identified with Apollonius of Tyna, but there is little evidence to connect him with the *Kitab Balabiyus*, and even if there was,the story implies that Balinas found the tablet rather than wrote it, and the recent discoveries of the dead sea scrolls and the nag hamamdi texts suggest that hiding texts in caves is not impossible, even if we did not have the pyramids before us. Ruska has suggested an origin further east, and Needham has proposed an origin in China.

Holmyard, Davis and Anon all consider that this Tablet may be one of the earliest of all alchemical works we have that survives.

It should be remarked that apparantly the Greeks and Egyptians used the term translated as `emerald' for emeralds, green granites, "and perhaps green jasper". In medieval times the emerald table of the Gothic kings of Spain, and the *Sacro Catino* - a dish said to have belonged to the Queen of Sheba, to have been used at the last supper, and to be made of emerald, were made of green glass

[Steele and Singer, 1928].

THE EMERALD TABLET OF HERMES & HIRAMIC LEGEND

The Emerald Tablet, the Most Ancient Monument of the Chaldeans
Concerning the Lapis Philosophoram

From: *The Lost Keys of Feemasonry.* Hall, Manly P. (1923)

The Emerald Tablet of Hermes (Tabula Smaragdina) introduces us to Hiram, the hero of the Masonic legend. The name Hiram is taken from the Chaldean Chiram. The first two words in large print mean the secret work. The second line in large letters - (CHIRAM TELAT MECHASOT - means Chiram, the Universal Agent, one in Essence, but three in aspect. Translated, the body of the Tablet reads as follows:

"It is true and no lie, certain, and to be depended upon, that the superior agrees with the inferior, and the inferior with the superior, to effect that one truly wonderful work. As all things owe their existence to the will of the Only One, so all things owe their origin to One Only Thing, the most hidden, by the arrangement of the Only God. The father of that One Only Thing is the Sun; its mother is the Moon; the wind carries it in its wings; but its nurse is a Spirituous Earth. That One Only Thing (after God) is the father of all things in the universe. Its power is perfect, after it has been united to a spirituous earth. Separate that spirituous earth from the dense or crude earth by means of a gentle heat, with much attention. In great measure it ascends from the earth up to heaven, and descends again, new born, on the earth, and the superior and inferior are increased in power. By this thou wilt partake of the honors of the whole world and darkness will fly from thee. This is the strength of all powers; with this thou wilt be able to overcome all things and to transmute all that is fine and all that is coarse. In this manner the world was created, but the arrangements to follow this road are hidden. For this reason I am called CHIRAM TELAT MECHASOT, one in Essence, but three in aspect. In this Trinity is hidden the wisdom of the whole world. It is ended now, what I have said concerning the effects of the Sun."

In a rare, unpublished old manuscript dealing with early Masonic and Hermetic mysteries, we find the following information concerning the mysterious universal agent referred to as "Chiram" (Hiram):

The sense of this emerald tablet can sufficiently convince us that the author was well acquainted with the secret operations of nature and with the secret work of the philosophers (alchemists and Hermetic philosophists). He likewise well knew and believed in the true God.

It has been believed since several ages that Cham, one of the sons of Noah, is the author of this monument of antiquity. A very ancient author, whose name is not known, who lived several centuries before Christ, mentions this tablet, and says that he had seen it in Egypt, at the court; that it was a precious stone, an emerald, whereon these characters were represented in bas relief, not engraved.

He states that it was in his time esteemed over two thousand years old, and that the matter of this emerald had once been in a fluid state like melted glass, and had been cast in a mold, and that to this flux the artist had given the hardness of a natural and genuine emerald, by art. (Alchemical art.)

The Canaanites were called the Phoenicians by the Greeks, who have told us that they had Hermes for one of their kings. There is a great relation between Chiram and Hermes.

Chiram is a word composed out of three words, denoting the universal spirit, the essence whereof the whole creation does consist, and the object of Chaldean, Egyptian and genuine natural philosophy, according to its inward principles or properties. The three Hebrew words Chuma, Ruach, and Majim, mean respectively Fire, Air, and Water, while their initial consonants, Ch, R, M, give us Chiram, that invisible essence which is the father of earth, fire, air and water, because, although immaterial in its own invisible nature, as the unmoved and electrical fire, when moved it becomes light and visible; and when collected and agitated, becomes heat and visible and tangible fire; and when it associates with humidity it becomes material.

The word Chiram has been metamorphosed into Hermes and also into Herman, and the translators of the Bible have made Hiram by changing Chet into He; both of these Hebrew word signs being very similar.

In the old word Hermaphrodite, a word invented by the philosophers, we find Hermes changed to Herm, signifying Chiram, or the universal agent, and Aphrodite, the passive principle of humidity, who is also called Venus, and is said to have been produced and generated by the sea.

We also read that Hiram (Chiram), or the universal agent, assisted King Solomon to build the temple; no doubt as Solomon possessed wisdom, he understood what to do with the corporealized universal agent. The Talmud of the Jews says that King Solomon built the temple by the assistance of Schamir. Now this word signifies the sun, as the large machine which is perpetually collecting the Omnipresent, surrounding, electrical fire, or Spiritus Mundi, and sends it constantly to us in the planets, in a visible manner called light.

This electrical flame, corporealized and regenerated into the stone of the philosophers, enabled King Solomon to produce the immense quantities of gold and silver used to build and decorate his temple.

These ancient paragraphs from an ancient philosopher may assist the student of today to realize the tremendous and undreamed-of store of knowledge that lies behind the allegory, which he often hears but seldom analyzes. Hiram, the universal agent, might be translated Vita, the power eternally building and unfolding the bodies of man. The use and abuse of energy is the key to this Masonic legend; in fact, it is the key to all things in nature. And Hiram, as the triple energy, one in source but three in aspect, can almost be called ether, the unknown hypothetical element, which carries the impulses of the gods through the macrocosmic nervous system of the Infinite. Hermes, or Mercury, was the messenger of the gods, and ether carries impulse upon its wings. The solving of the mystery of ether, or, if you prefer to call it such, 'vibrant space', is the great problem of Masonry. This ether, as a hypothetical medium, brings energy to the three bodies of thought, emotion, and action, and in this way Chiram, the one in essence, becomes three in aspect - mental, emotional, and vital.

GLORY OF THE WORLD

It is true, without any error, and it is the sum of truth; that which is above is also that which is below, for the performance of the wonders of a certain one thing, and as all things arise from one Stone, so also they were generated from one common Substance, which includes the four elements created by God. And among other miracles the said Stone is born of the First Matter. The Sun is its Father, the Moon its Mother, the wind bears it in its womb, and it is nursed by the earth. Itself is the Father of the whole earth, and the whole potency thereof. If it be transmuted into earth, then the earth separates from the fire that which is most subtle from that which is hard, operating gently and with great artifice. Then the Stone ascends from earth to heaven, and again descends from heaven to earth, and receives the choicest influences of both heaven and earth. If you can perform this you have the glory of the world, and are able to put to flight all diseases, and to transmute all metals. It overcomes Mercury, which is subtle, and penetrates all hard and solid bodies. Hence it is compared with the world. Hence I am called Hermes, having the three parts of the whole world of philosophy.

Explanation of the Emerald Table of Hermes.

Hermes is right in saying that our Art is true, and has been rightly handed down by the Sages; all doubts concerning it have arisen through false interpretation of the mystic language of the philosophers. But, since they are loth to confess their own ignorance, their readers prefer to say that the words of the Sages are imposture and falsehood. The fault really lies with the ignorant reader, who does not understand the style of the Philosophers. If, in the interpretation of our books, they would suffer themselves to be guided by the teaching of Nature, rather than by their own foolish notions, they would not miss the mark so hopelessly.

By the words which follow: "That which is above is also that which is below," he describes the Matter of our Art, which, though one, is divided into two things, the volatile water which rises upward, and the earth which lies at the bottom, and becomes fixed. But when the reunion takes place, the body becomes spirit, and the spirit becomes body, the earth is changed into water and becomes volatile, the water is transmuted into body, and becomes fixed. When bodies become spirits, and spirits bodies, your work is finished, for then that which rises upward and that which descends downward become one body. Therefore the Sage says that that which is above is that which is below, meaning that, after having been separated into two substances (from being one substance), they are again joined together into one substance, i.e., an union which can never be dissolved, and possesses such virtue and efficacy that it can do in one moment what the Sun cannot accomplish in a thousand years. And this miracle is wrought by a thing which is despised and rejected by the multitude.

Again, the Sage tells us that all things were created, and are still generated, from one first substance and consist of the same elementary material; and in this first substance God has appointed the four elements, which represent a common material into which it might perhaps be possible to resolve all things. Its development is brought about by the distillation of the Sun and Moon. For it is operated upon by the natural heat of the Sun and Moon, which stirs up its internal action, and multiplies each thing after its kind, imparting to the substance a specific form. The soul, or nutritive principle, is the earth which receives the rays of the Sun and Moon, and therewith feeds her children as with mother's milk. Thus the Sun is the father, the Moon is the mother, the earth the nurse – and in this substance is that which we require. He who can take it and prepare it is truly to be envied.

It is separated by the Sun and Moon in the form of a vapour, and collected in the place where it is found. When Hermes adds that "the air bears it in its womb, the earth is its nurse, the whole world its Father," he means that when the substance of our Stone is dissolved, then the wind bears it in its womb, i.e., the air bears up the substance in the form of water, in which is hid fire, the soul of the Stone, and fire is the Father of the whole world. Thus, the volatile substance rises upward, while that which remains at the bottom, is the "whole world" (seeing that our Art is compared to a "small world "). Hence Hermes calls fire the father of the whole world, because it is the Sun of our Art, and air, Moon, and water ascend from it; the earth is the nurse of the Stone, i.e., when the earth receives the rays of the Sun and Moon, a new body is born, like a new foetus in the mother's womb. The earth receives and digests the light of Sun and Moon, and imparts food to its foetus day by day, till it becomes great and strong, and puts off its blackness and defilement, and is changed to a different colour.

This "child,"which is called "our daughter," represents our Stone, which is born anew of the Sun and Moon, as you may easily see, when the spirit, or the water that ascended, is gradually transmuted into the body, and the body is born anew, and grows and increases in size like the foetus in the mother's womb.

Thus the Stone is generated from the first substance, which contains the four elements; it is brought forth by two things, the body and the spirit; the wind bears it in its womb, for it carries the Stone upward from earth to heaven, and down again from heaven to earth. Thus the Stone receives increase from above and from below, and is born a second time, just as every other foetus is generated in the maternal womb; as all created things bring forth their young, even so does the air, or wind, bring forth our Stone. When Hermes adds, "Its power, or virtue, is entire, when it is transmuted into earth," he means that when the spirit is transmuted into the body, it receives its full strength and virtue. For as yet the spirit is volatile, and not fixed, or permanent. If it is to be fixed, we must proceed as the baker does in baking bread. We must impart only a little of the spirit to the body at a time, just as the baker only puts a little leaven to his meal, and with it leavens the whole lump. The spirit, which is our leaven, in like fashion transmutes the whole body into its own substance. Therefore the body must be leavened again and again, until the whole lump is thoroughly pervaded with the power of the leaven. In our Art the body leavens the spirit, and transmutes it into one body, and the spirit leavens the body, and transmutes it into one spirit. And the two, when they have become one, receive power to leaven all things, into which they are injected, with their own virtue.

The Sage continues: "If you gently separate the earth from the water, the subtle from the hard, the Stone ascends from earth to heaven, and again descends from heaven to earth, and receives its virtue from above and from below. By this process you obtain the glory and brightness of the whole world. With it you can put to flight poverty, disease, and weariness; for it overcomes the subtle mercury, and penetrates all hard and firm bodies."

He means that all who would accomplish this task must separate the moist from the dry, the water from the earth. The water, or fire, being subtle, ascends, while the body is hard, and remains where it is. The separation must be accomplished by gentle heat, i.e., in the temperate bath of the Sages, which acts slowly, and is neither too hot nor too cold. Then the Stone ascends to heaven, and again descends from heaven to earth. The spirit and body are first separated, then again joined together by gentle coction, of a temperature resembling that with which a hen hatches her eggs. Such is the preparation of the substance, which is worth the whole world, whence it is also called a "little world." The possession of the Stone will yield you the greatest delight, and unspeakably precious comfort. It will also set forth to you in a typical form the creation of the world. It will enable you to cast out all disease from the human body, to drive away poverty, and to have a good understanding of the secrets of Nature. The Stone has virtue to transmute mercury into gold and silver, and to penetrate all hard and firm bodies, such as precious stones and metals. You cannot ask a better gift of God than this gift, which is greater than all other gifts.

Hence Hermes may justly call himself by the proud title of "Hermes Trismegistus, who holds the three parts of the whole world of wisdom."

TRANSLATIONS

From Jabir ibn Hayyan.

0) Balinas mentions the engraving on the table in the hand of Hermes, which says:

1) Truth! Certainty! That in which there is no doubt!

2) That which is above is from that which is below, and that which is below is from that which is above, working the miracles of one.

3) As all things were from one.

4) Its father is the Sun and its mother the Moon.

5) The Earth carried it in her belly, and the Wind nourished it in her belly,

7) as Earth which shall become Fire.

7a) Feed the Earth from that which is subtle, with the greatest power.

8) It ascends from the earth to the heaven and becomes ruler over that which is above and that which is below.

14) And I have already explained the meaning of the whole of this in two of these books of mine.

[Holmyard 1923: 562.]

Another Arabic Version (from the German of Ruska, translated by 'Anonymous').

0) Here is that which the priest Sagijus of Nabulus has dictated concerning the entrance of Balinas into the hidden chamber... After my entrance into the chamber, where the talisman was set up, I came up to an old man sitting on a golden throne, who was holding an emerald tablet in one hand. And behold the following - in Syriac, the primordial language - was written thereon:

1) Here (is) a true explanation, concerning which there can be no doubt.

2) It attests: The above from the below, and the below from the above - the work of the miracle of the One.

3) And things have been from this primal substance through a single act. How wonderful is this work! It is the main (principle) of the world and is its maintainer.

4) Its father is the sun and its mother the moon;

5) the wind has borne it in its body, and the earth has nourished it.

6) the father of talismen and the protector of miracles

6a) whose powers are perfect, and whose lights are confirmed (?),

7) a fire that becomes earth.

7a) Separate the earth from the fire, so you will attain the subtle as more inherent than the gross, with care and sagacity.

8) It rises from earth to heaven, so as to draw the lights of the heights to itself,

and descends to the earth; thus within it are the forces of the above and the below; 9) because the light of lights within it, thus does the darkness flee before it.

10) The force of forces, which overcomes every subtle thing and penetrates into everything gross.

11) The structure of the microcosm is in accordance with the structure of the macrocosm.

12) And accordingly proceed the knowledgeable.

13) And to this aspired Hermes, who was threefold graced with wisdom.

14) And this is his last book, which he concealed in the chamber.

[Anon 1985: 24-5]

Twelfth Century Latin

0) When I entered into the cave, I received the tablet zaradi, which was inscribed, from between the hands of Hermes, in which I discovered these words:

1) True, without falsehood, certain, most certain.

2) What is above is like what is below, and what is below is like that which is above. To make the miracle of the one thing.

3) And as all things were made from contemplation of one, so all things were born from one adaptation.

4) Its father is the Sun, its mother is the Moon.

5) The wind carried it in its womb, the earth breast-fed it.

6) It is the father of all 'works of wonder' (Telesmi) in the world.

6a) Its power is complete (integra).

7) If cast to (turned towards - versa fuerit) earth,

7a) it will separate earth from fire, the subtile from the gross.

8) With great capacity it ascends from earth to heaven. Again it descends to earth, and takes back the power of the above and the below.

9) Thus you will receive the glory of the distinctiveness of the world. All obscurity will flee from you.

10) This is the whole most strong strength of all strength, for it overcomes all subtle things, and penetrates all solid things.

11a) Thus was the world created.

12) From this comes marvelous adaptions of which this is the proceedure.

13) Therefore I am called Hermes, because I have three parts of the wisdom of the whole world.

14) And complete is what I had to say about the work of the Sun, from the book of Galieni Alfachimi.

[From Latin in Steele and Singer 1928]

Aurelium Occultae Philosophorum. Georgio Beato

1) This is true and remote from all cover of falsehood
2) Whatever is below is similar to that which is above. Through this the marvels of the work of one thing are procured and perfected.
3) Also, as all things are made from one, by the condsideration of one, so all things were made from this one, by conjunction.
4) The father of it is the sun, the mother the moon.
5) The wind bore it in the womb. Its nurse is the earth, the mother of all perfection.
6a)Its power is perfected.
7) If it is turned into earth,
7a) separate the earth from the fire, the subtle and thin from the crude and course, prudently, with modesty and wisdom.
8) This ascends from the earth into the sky and again descends from the sky to the earth, and receives the power and efficacy of things above and of things below.
9) By this means you will acquire the glory of the whole world, and so you will drive away all shadows and blindness.
10) For this by its fortitude snatches the palm from all other fortitude and power. For it is able to penetrate and subdue everything subtle and everything crude and hard.
11a) By this means the world was founded
12) and hence the marvelous cojunctions of it and admirable effects, since this is the way by which these marvels may be brought about.
13) And because of this they have called me Hermes Tristmegistus since I have the three parts of the wisdom and Philsosphy of the whole universe.
14) My speech is finished which i have spoken concerning the solar work

[Davis 1926: 874.]

Translation of Isaac Newton c. 1680.

1) Tis true without lying, certain & most true.
2) That wch is below is like that wch is above & that wch is above is like yt wch is below to do ye miracles of one only thing.
3) And as all things have been & arose from one by ye mediation of one: so all things have their birth from this one thing by adaptation.
4) The Sun is its father, the moon its mother,
5) the wind hath carried it in its belly, the earth its nourse.
6) The father of all perfection in ye whole world is here.
7) Its force or power is entire if it be converted into earth.

7a) Seperate thou ye earth from ye fire, ye subtile from the gross sweetly wth great indoustry.

8) It ascends from ye earth to ye heaven & again it desends to ye earth and receives ye force of things superior & inferior.

9) By this means you shall have ye glory of ye whole world & thereby all obscurity shall fly from you.

10) Its force is above all force. ffor it vanquishes every subtile thing & penetrates every solid thing.

11a) So was ye world created.

12) From this are & do come admirable adaptaions whereof ye means (Or process) is here in this.

13) Hence I am called Hermes Trismegist, having the three parts of ye philosophy of ye whole world.

14) That wch I have said of ye operation of ye Sun is accomplished & ended.

[Dobbs 1988: 183-4.]

Translation from Kriegsmann, alledgedly from the Phoenician

1) I speak truly, not falsely, certainly and most truly

2) These things below with those above and those with these join forces again so that they produce a single thing the most wonderful of all.

3) And as the whole universe was brought forth from one by the word of one GOD, so also all things are regenerated perpetually from this one according to the disposition of Nature.

4) It has the Sun for father and the Moon for mother:

5) it is carried by the air as if in a womb, it is nursed by the earth.

6) It is the cause, this, of all perfection of all things throughout the universe.

6a) This will attain the highest perfection of powers

7) if it shall be reduced into earth

7a) Distribute here the earth and there the fire, thin out the density of this the suavest (suavissima) thing of all.

8) Ascend with the greatest sagacity of genius from the earth into the sky, and thence descend again to the earth, and recognise that the forces of things above and of things below are one,

9) so as to posses the glory of the whole world - and beyond this man of abject fate may have nothing further.

10) This thing itself presently comes forth stronger by reasons of this fortitude: it subdues all bodies surely, whether tenuous or solid, by penetrating them.

11a) And so everything whatsoever that the world contains was created.

12) Hence admirable works are accomplished which are instituted (carried out - instituuntur) according to the same mode.

13) To me therefor the name of Hermes Trismegistus has been awarded because I am discovered as the Teacher of the three parts of the wisdom of the world.

14) These then are the considerations which I have concluded ought to be written down concerning the readiest operations of the Chymic art.

[Davis 1926: 875 slightly modified.]

From Sigismund Bacstrom (allegedly translated from Chaldean).

0) The Secret Works of CHIRAM - ONE in essence, but three in aspect.

1) It is true, no lie, certain and to be depended upon,

2) the superior agrees with the inferior, and the inferior agrees with the superior, to effect that one truly wonderful work.

3) As all things owe their existence to the will of the only one, so all things owe their origin to the one only thing, the most hidden by the arrangement of the only God.

4) The father of that one only thing is the sun its mother is the moon,

5) the wind carries it in its belly; but its nourse is a spirituous earth.

6) That one only thing is the father of all things in the Universe.

6a) Its power is perfect,

7) after it has been united with a spirituous earth.

7a) Separate that spirituous earth from the dense or crude by means of a gentle heat, with much attention.

8) In great measure it ascends from the earth up to heaven, and descends again, newborn, on the earth, and the superior and the inferior are increased in power.

9) By this wilt thou partake of the honours of the whole world. And Darkness will fly from thee.

10) This is the strength of all powers. With this thou wilt be able to overcome all things and transmute all what is fine and what is coarse.

11a) In this manner the world was created;

12) the arrangements to follow this road are hidden.

13) For this reason I am called Chiram Telat Mechasot, one in essence, but three in aspect. In this trinity is hidden the wisdom of the whole world.

14) It is ended now, what I have said concerning the effects of the sun.

Finish of the Tabula Smaragdina.

[See Hall, 1923]

From Madame Blavatsky

2) What is below is like that which is above, and what is above is similar to that which is below to accomplish the wonders of the one thing.

3) As all things were produced by the mediation of one being, so all things were produced from this one by adaption.

4) Its father is the sun, its mother the moon.

6a) It is the cause of all perfection throughout the whole earth.

7) Its power is perfect if it is changed into earth.

7a) Separate the earth from the fire, the subtle from the gross, acting prudently and with judgement.

8) Ascend with the greatest sagacity from earth to heaven, and unite together the power of things inferior and superior;

9) thus you will possess the light of the whole world, and all obscurity will fly away from you.

10) This thing has more fortitude than fortitude itself, because it will overcome every subtile thing and penetrate every solid thing.

11a) By it the world was formed.

[Blavatsky, 1877]

From Fulcanelli (translated from the French by Sieveking)

1) This is the truth, the whole truth and nothing but the truth:-

2) As below, so above; and as above so below. With this knowledge alone you may work miracles.

3) And since all things exist in and eminate from the ONE Who is the ultimate Cause, so all things are born after their kind from this ONE.

4) The Sun is the father, the Moon the mother;

5) the wind carried it in his belly. Earth is its nurse and its guardian.

6) It is the Father of all things,

6a) the eternal Will is contained in it.

7) Here, on earth, its strength, its power remain one and undivided.

7a) Earth must be separated from fire, the subtle from the dense, gently with unremitting care.

8) It arises from the earth and descends from heaven; it gathers to itself the strength of things above and things below.

9) By means of this one thing all the glory of the world shall be yours and all obscurity flee from you.

10) It is power, strong with the strength of all power, for it will penetrate all mysteries and dispel all ignorance.

11a) By it the world was created.

12) From it are born manifold wonders, the means to achieving which are here given

13) It is for this reason that I am called Hermes Trismegistus; for I possess the three essentials of the philosophy of the universe.

14) This is is the sum total of the work of the Sun.

[Sadoul 1972: 25-6.]

From Fulcanelli, new translation

1) It is true without untruth, certain and most true:

2) that which is below is like that which is on high, and that which is on high is like that which is below; by these things are made the miracles of one thing.

3) And as all things are, and come from One, by the mediation of One, So all things are born from this unique thing by adaption.

4) The Sun is the father and the Moon the mother.

5) The wind carries it in its stomach. The earth is its nourisher and its receptacle.

6 The Father of all the Theleme of the universal world is here.

6a) Its force, or power, remains entire,

7) if it is converted into earth.

7a) You separate the earth from the fire, the subtle from the gross, gently with great industry.

8) It climbs from the earth and descends from the sky, and receives the force of things superior and things inferior.

9) You will have by this way, the glory of the world and all obscurity will flee from you.

10) It is the power strong with all power, for it will defeat every subtle thing and penetrate every solid thing

11a) In this way the world was created.

12) From it are born wonderful adaptations, of which the way here is given.

13) That is why I have been called Hermes Tristmegistus, having the three parts of the universal philosophy.

14) This, that I have called the solar Work, is complete.

[Translated from Fulcanelli 1964: 312.]

From Idres Shah

1) The truth, certainty, truest, without untruth.

2)What is above is like what is below. What is below is like what is above. The miracle of unity is to be attained.

3) Everything is formed from the contemplation of unity, and all things come about from unity, by means of adaptation.

4) Its parents are the Sun and Moon.

5) It was borne by the wind and nurtured by the Earth.

6) Every wonder is from it

6a) and its power is complete.

7) Throw it upon earth,

7a) and earth will separate from fire. The impalpable separated from the palpable.

8) Through wisdom it rises slowly from the world to heaven. Then it descends to the world combining the power of the upper and the lower.

9)Thus you will have the illumination of all the world, and darkness will disappear.

10) This is the power of all strength - it overcomes that which is delicate and penetrates through solids.

11a) This was the means of the creation of the world.

12) And in the future wonderful developments will be made, and this is the way.

13) I am Hermes the Threefold Sage, so named because I hold the three elements of all wisdom.

14) And thus ends the revelation of the work of the Sun.

(Shah 1964: 198).

Hypothetical Chinese Original

1) True, true, with no room for doubt, certain, worthy of all trust.

2) See, the highest comes from the lowest, and the lowest from the highest; indeed a marvelous work of the tao.

3) See how all things originated from It by a single process.

4) The father of it (the elixir) is the sun (Yang), its mother the moon (Yin).

5) The wind bore it in its belly, and the earth nourished it.

6)This is the father of wondrous works (changes and transformations), the guardian of mysteries,

6a) perfect in its powers, the animator of lights.

7) This fire will be poured upon the earth...

7a) So separate the earth from the fire, the subtle from the gross, acting prudently and with art.

8) It ascends from the earth to the heavens (and orders the lights above), then descends again to the earth; and in it is the power of the highest and the lowest.

9) Thus when you have the light of lights darkness will flee away from you.

10) With this power of powers (the elixir) you shall be able to get the mastery of every subtle thing, and be able to penetrate everything that is gross.

11a) In this way was the great world itself formed.

12) Hence thus and thus marvellous operations will be acheived.

[after Needham 1980: 371.]

TEXTUAL REMARKS

On #3
Some Latin texts have meditatione (contemplation), others mediatione (mediation). Some texts have adaptatione (by adaptation), some have adoptionis (by adoption).

On #6
'Telesmi' is a greek word, some texts have 'thelesmi'.

On #6, 7
In some texts 'Its Power is Complete' is a separate line. In the generally accepted reading, this runs into #7 producing 'Its Power is complete if versa fuerit to earth'. Where possible this has been indicated by dividing these lines in 6, 6a, 7, & 7a

On #7, 8
In some texts the 'Wisdom, capacity' (magno ingenio) is read as referring to #7, and hence the operation of Separation is to be carried out 'carefully', in other readings the 'wisdom' is held to refer to #8 and the product of the Separation which thus ascends with 'wisdom'.

Needham quotes Ruska to the effect that sections 3, 12 and 14 are probably late additions (op. cit.)

COMMENTARIES

On #1
Hortulanus: "... the most true Sun is procreated by art. And he says most true in the superlative degree because the Sun generated by this art exceeds all natural Sun in all of its properties, medicinal and otherwise" (Davis modified by `Linden')

On #2
Albertus Magnus: Hermes says "the powers of all things below originate in the stars and constellations of the heavens: and that all these powers are poured down into all things below by the circle called Alaur, which is, they said, the first circle of the constellations". This descent is "noble when the materials receiving these powers are more like things above in their brightness and transparency; ignoble when the materials are confused and foul, so that the heavenly power is, as it were oppressed. Therefore they say that this is the reason why precious

stones more than anything else have wonderful powers" (60 -61). While the "seven kinds of metals have their forms from the seven planets of the lower spheres" (168).

Hortulanus: "the stone is divided into two principle parts by the magistry, into a superior part which ascends above and into an inferior part which remains below fixed and clear. And these two parts moreover are concordant in their virtue since the inferior part is earth which is called nurse and ferment, and the superior part is the spirit which quickens the whole stone and raises it up. Wherefore separation made, and conjunction celebrated, many miracles are effected."

Burckhardt: "This refers to the reciprocal dependence of the active and the passive... essential form cannot be manifested without passive materia... the efficacy of the spiritual power depends on the preparedness of the human 'container' and vice versa.... 'Above' and 'below' are thus related to this one thing and complement one another in its regard".

Schumaker: "There are corresponding planes in various levels of creation, hence it is safe to draw analogies between macrocosm and microcosm, the mineral kingdom and the human, animal and vegetable kingdoms etc".

Needham: "the whole affirmation looks remarkably like the doctrine that extreme of Yang generates Yin, and vice versa".

On #3

Hortulanus: "our stone, which was created by God, was born and came forth from a confused mass, containing in itself all the elements - and hence our stone was born by this single miracle".

Trithemius: "Is it not true that all things flow from one thing, from the goodness of the One, and that whatever is joined to Unity cannot be diverse, but rather fructifies by means of the simplicity and adaptability of the One" "What is born from Unity? Is it not the ternary? Take note: Unity is unmixed, the binary is compounded, and the ternary is reduced to the simplicity of Unity. I, Trithemius, am not of three minds, but persist in a single integrated mind taking pleasure in the ternary, which gives birth to a marvelous offspring" (Bran)

Burckhardt: "the undivided, invisible Light of the unconditioned One is refracted into multiplicity by the prism of the Spirit". As the Spirit contemplates the Unity without full comprehension "it manifests the 'many-sided' All, just as a lens transmits the light it receives as a bundle of rays".

Schumaker: As God is one, all created objects come from one thing, an undifferentiated primal matter.

On #4

Hortulanus: "As one animal naturally generates more animals similar to itself, so the Sun artificially generates Sun by the power of multiplication of...the stone.... in this artificial generation it is necessary that the Sun have a suitable receptacle, consonant with itself, for its sperm and its tincture, and this is the Luna of the philosophers."

Redgrove: Sun and Moon "probably stand for Spirit and Matter respectively, not gold and silver".

Burckhardt: Sun "is the spirit (nous), while the moon is the soul (psyche)".

Schumaker: "If the moon is associated with water, as because of its 'moisture' [as] was usual, and the sun with fire, the prima materia is understood to have been generated by fire, born of water, brought down from the sky by wind, and nourished by earth".

On #5

Albertus Magnus: by this Hermes "means the levigatio [making light weight] of the material, raising it to the properties of Air. And why he says the wind carries the material [of the stone] in its belly is that, when the material is placed in an alembic- which is a vessel made like those in which rosewater is prepared - then by evapouration it is rendered subtle and is raised towards the properties of Air... And there distills and issues from the mouth of the alembic a watery or oily liquor with all the powers of the elements". In metals the moisture is not separated from the dryness, but is dissolved in it; and being so dissolved, it moves about there as if it had been swallowed by the Earth and were moving about in its bowels. And on this account Hermes said 'The mother of metal is Earth that carries it in her belly'".

Hortulanus: "It is plain that wind is air, and air is life, and life is spirit... And thus it is necessary that the wind should bear the whole stone.... [However] our stone without the ferment of the earth will never come to the effect, which ferment is called food"

Trithemius: "the wind carries its seed in her belly".

Maier: By "the wind carried him in its belly" Hermes means " 'He, whose father is the Sun, and whose mother is the Moon, will be carried before he is born, by wind and vapour, just as a flying bird is carried by air'. From the vapours of winds, which are nothing else but wind in motion, water proceeds, when condensed, and from that water, mixed with earth, all minerals and metals arise". The substance carried by the wind is "in chemical respect.. the sulphur, which is carried in mercury". Lull says "'The stone is the fire, carried in the belly of the air'. In physical respect it is the unborn child that will soon be born". To be clearer, "All mercury is composed of vapours, that is to say of water, which the earth raises along with it into the thin air, and of earth, which the air compels to return into watery earth or earthy water" As the elements contained within are each reduced to a watery condition, they either follow the volatile elements upward as in common mercury, or they stay below with the solid elements as in philosophical Mercury "and in the solid metals". So "Mercury is the wind which receives the sulphur... as the unripe fruit from the mothers womb, or from the ashes of the burnt mother's body and takes it to a place where it may ripen". Ripley says "our child shall be born in the air, that is the belly of the wind" [de Jong 1969: 55- 7.]

Maier (2nd Comment) on "The earth is its nurse": Food changes into the substance of the eater and is then assimilated. "This harmony dominates the whole of nature, for the like enjoys the like". The same happens in the Work and Nature "just as is the growth of the child in the mother's womb. So also a father, a mother and a nurse have been attributed to the philosophical child... it comes into being from the twofold seed and then grows as an embryo does". As a woman must moderate her diet to avoid miscarriage, "in the same way one must set about philosophical work with moderation". The Seeds also have to be united. "Philosophers say that the one comes from the East and the other from the West and become one; what does this mean but combining in a retort, a moderate temperature and nourishment?". "One may wonder why the earth is referred to as the nurse of the philosophic child, since barreness and dryness are the main properties of the element earth". The answer is that not the element, but the whole Earth is meant. "It is the nurse of Heaven not because it resolves, washes and moistens the foetus, but because it coagulates, fastens and colours the latter and changes it into sap and blood... The Earth contains a wonderful juice which changes the nature of the one who feeds on it, as Romulus is believed to have been changed by the wolf's milk into a bellicose individual" [de Jong 1969: 63 -5.]

Burckhardt: "The wind which carries the spiritual germ in its body, is the vital breath". Vital breath is the substance of the realm between heaven and earth, it "is also Quicksilver which contains the germ of gold in a liquid state". The earth is "the body, as an inward reality".

On #6
Burckhardt: the word talisman is derived from Telesma. Talismans work by corresponding to their prototype, and by making a "'condensation', on the subtle

plane, of a spiritual state. This explains the similarity between the talisman, as the bearer of an invisible influence, and the alchemical elixir, as the 'ferment' of metallic transformation".

On #7

Hortulanus: The stone is perfect and complete if it is turned into earth "that is if the soul of the stone itself.... is turned into earth, namely of the stone and is fixed so that the whole substance of the stone becomes one with its nurse, namely the earth, and the whole stone is converted to ferment"

Trithemius: it is the seed from #5 that must be cast upon the earth.

Bacstrom: "Process - First Distillation".

Burckhardt: "when the Spirit is 'embodied', the volatile becomes fixed".

Schumaker: if the prime matter is to be used it must be fixed into a substance "capable of being handled".

On #7a

Hortulanus: "You will separate, that is, you will dissolve, because solution is separation of parts.."

Burkhardt: The separation "means the 'extraction' of the soul from the body".

Schumaker "Since the volatile principle is fire - or sometimes, air - stability is produced by its removal. Or, alternatively but less probably, the earth is impurity ('the gross') and a purified fire ('the subtle') is what is wanted.

On #8

Albertus Magnus: In intending to teach the operations of alchemy Hermes says the stone "'ascends to heaven' when by roasting and calcination it takes on the properties of Fire; for alchemists mean by *calcinatio* the reduction of material to powder by burning and roasting. And the material 'again descends from heaven to earth' when it takes on the properties of Earth by *inhumatio*, for inhumation revives and nourishes what was previously killed by calcination".

Hortulanus: "And now he deals with multiplication [of the stone]." "Although our stone is divided in the first operation into four parts... there are really two principle parts". The ascending, non fixed, and the earth or ferment. "It is necessary to have a large quantity of this non fixed part and to give it to the stone which has been made thoroughly clean from dirt.... until the entire stone is borne above by the virtue of the spirit"
"Afterwards it is necessary to incerate the same stone,..with the oil that was

extracted in the first operation, which oil is called 'the water of the stone.'"
Roast or boil by sublimation until the "entire stone descends... and remains fixed
and fluent". "That which is coporeal is made spiritual by sublimation, and that
which is spiritual is made corporeal by descension".

Trithemius: "When the ternary has at last returned to itself it may, by an inner
disposition and great delight, ascend from the earth to heaven, thereby receiving
both superior and inferior power; thus will it be made powerful and glorious in
the clarity of Unity, demonstrate its ability to bring forth every number, and put
to flight all obscurity".

Bacstrom: "Last Digestion". "The Azoth ascends from the Earth, from the
bottom of the Glass, and redescends in Veins and drops into the Earth, and by
this continual circulation the Azoth is more and more subtilised, Volatilizes Sol
and carries the volatilized Solar atoms along with it and thereby becomes a Solar
Azoth, i.e. our third and genuine Sophic Mercury". The circulation must continue
until "it ceases of itself, and the Earth has sucked it all in, when it becomes the
black pitchy matter, the Toad [the substances in the alchemical retort and also the
lower elements in the body of man - Hall], which denotes complete putrifaction
or Death of the compound".

Read, suggests this section describes the use of a kerotakis, in which metals are
suspended and subject to the action of gasses released from substances heated in
the base, and from their condensation and circulation.

Burckhardt: "dissolution of consciousness from all formal 'coagulations'
is followed by the 'crystalisation' of the Spirit, so that active and passive are
perfectly united."

Schumaker: "Separate the volatile part of the substance by vaporization but
continue heating until the vapour reunites with the parent body, whereupon you
will have obtained the Stone".

On #9
Trithemius: When the ternary has returned to Unity cleansed of all impurities
"the mind understands without contradiction all the mysteries of the excellently
arranged arcanum".

Bacstrom: the black matter becomes White and Red. The Red "having been
carried to perfection, medicinaly and for Metals" is capable of supporting
complete mental and physical health, and provides "ample means, *in finitum
multiplicable* to be benevolent and charitable, without any dimunation of our
inexhaustable resources, therefore well may it be called the Glory of the whole

World". Contemplation and study of the Philosopher's Stone ("L. P.") elevates the mind to God. "The Philosophers say with great Truth, that the L.P. either finds a good man or makes one". "By invigorating the Organs the Soul makes use of for communicating with exterior objects, the Soul must aquire greater powers, not only for conception but also for retention". If we pray and have faith "all Obscurity must vanish of course".

Burckhardt: "Thus the light of the Spirit becomes constant... [and] ignorance, deception, uncertainty, doubt and foolishness will be removed from consciousness".

On #10
Trithemius: The Philosopher's Stone is another name for the 'one thing', and is able to "conquer every subtile thing and to penetrate every solid". "This very noble virtue... consists of maximal fortitude, touching everything with its desirable excellence".

Bacstrom: "The L.P. does possess all the Powers concealed in Nature, not for destruction but for exhaltation and regeneration of matter, in the three Departments of Nature". "It refixes the most subtil Oxygen into its own firey Nature". The power increases "in a tenfold ratio, at every multiplication". So it can penetrate Gold and Silver, and fix mercury, Crystals and Glass Fluxes.

Burckhardt: "Alchemical fixation is nevertheless more inward... Through its union with the spirit bodily consciousness itself becomes a fine and penetrating power". He quotes Jabir "The body becomes a spirit, and takes on... fineness, lightness, extensibility, coloration... The spirit... becomes a body and aquires the latter's resistance to fire, immobility and duration. From both bodies a light substance is born , which.. precisely takes up a middle position between the two extremes".

Schumaker: The product of the distillation and reunion will "dominate less solid substances, but because of its own subtlety it will 'penetrate' and hence dominate, other solid things less pure and quasi-spiritual than itself".

On #11
Burckhardt: "the little world is created according to the prototype of the great world", when the human realises their original nature is the image of God.

Schumaker: "The alchemical operation is a paradigm of the creative process. We may note the sexual overtones of what has preceeded"

On #12

Burckhardt: "In the Arabic text this is: "This way is traversed by the sages"".

On #13

Hortulanus: "He here teaches in an occult manner the things from which the stone is made." "the stone is called perfect because it has in itself the nature of minerals, of vegetables and of animals. For the stone is three and one, triple and single, having four natures.... and three colours, namely black, white and red. It is also called the grain of corn because unless it shall have died, it remains itself alone. And if it shall have died... it bears much fruit when it is in conjunction..."

Newton: "on account of this art Mercurius is called thrice greatest, having three parts of the philosophy of the whole world, since he signifies the Mercury of the philosophers.... and has dominion in the mineral kingdom, the vegetable kingdom, and the animal kingdom".

Bacstrom: the wisdom of the world (?) is hidden in "Chiram and its Use". Hermes "signifies a Serpent, and the Serpent used to be an Emblem of Knowledge or Wisdom."

Burckhardt: "The three parts of wisdom correspond to the three great divisions of the universe, namely, the spiritual, psychic and corporeal realms, whose symbols are heaven, air and earth".

Schumaker: "The usual explanation of Tristmegistus.. is that Hermes was the greatest philosopher, the greatest priest, and the greatest king".

General

Trithemius: "our philosophy is celestial, not worldly, in order that we may faithfuly behold, by means of a direct intuition of the mind through faith and knowledge, that principle which we call God...."

Trithemius: "Study generates knowledge; knowledge prepares love; love, similarity; similarity, communion; communion, virtue; virtue, dignity; dignity, power; and power performs the miracle".

Newton "Inferior and superior, fixed and volatile, sulphur and quicksilver have a similar nature and are one thing, like man and wife. For they differ from one another only by degree of digestion and maturity. Sulphur is mature quicksilver, and quicksilver is immature sulphur: and on account of this affinity they unite like male and female, and they act on each other, and through that action they are mutually transmuted into each other and procreate a more noble offspring to accomplish the miracles of this one thing". "And just as all things were created from one Chaos by the design of one God, so in our art all things... are born from this one thing which is our Chaos, by the design of the Artificer and the skilful adaptation of things. And the generation of this is similar to the human, truly from a father and mother".

Blavatsky: the mysterious thing "is the universal, magical agent, the astral light, which in the correlations of its forces furnishes the alkahest, the philosopher's stone, and the elixir of life. Hermetic philosophy names it Azoth, the soul of the world, the celestial virgin, the great Magnes, etc" It appears to be that which gives organisation ("the maze of force-correlations"), and form i.e., the perfect geometry of snowflakes.

Sherwood Taylor: "the operation of the Sun... was carried out by a 'spirit', universal, the source of all things, having the power of perfecting them. Its virtue is integral [# 6a] (i.e., having the power to convert the diverse into a single substance), if it be turned into earth (i.e., solidified). This conveyed that the Stone was to be a solidified pneuma. Pneuma was the link between earth and heaven, having the virtue of the celestial and subterranean regions - the power of the whole cosmos from the fixed stars to the centre of the earth. It overcomes every nature and penetrates every solid. It is the source of the whole world and so it can be the means of changing things in a wonderful way. The three parts of the philosophy of the whole world are presumably of the celestial, terrestrial, and subterranean regions".

Shah: The table is "the same as the Sufi dictum... 'Man is the microcosm, creation the macrocosm - the unity. All comes from One. By the joining of the power of contemplation all can be attained. This essence must be separated from the body first, then combined with the body. This is the Work. Start with yourself, end with all. Before man, beyond man, transformation'".

A Commentary Of Ibn Umail

Hermus said the secret of everything and the life of everything is Water.... This water becomes in wheat, ferment; in the vine, wine; in the olive, olive oil.... The begining of the child is from water.... Regarding this spiritual water and the sanctified and thirsty earth, Hermus the great, crowned with the glorious wisdom and the sublime sciences, said [#1] Truth it is, indubtible, certain and correct,

[#2] that the High is from the Low and the Low is from the High. They bring about wonders through the one, just as things are produced from that one essence by a single preparation. Later by his statement [#4] Its father is the Sun and its mother the Moon he meant their male and their female. They are the two birds which are linked together in the pictures given regarding the beginning of the operation, and from them the spiritual tinctures are produced. And similarly they are at the end of the operation. Later in his statement [#7 ?] the subtle is more honourable than the gross, he means by the subtle the divine spiritual water; and by the gross the earthly body. As for his later statement [#8] with gentleness and wisdom it will ascend from the earth to the sky, and will take fire from the higher lights, he means by this the distillation and the raising of the water into the air. As for his later statement [#8a] It will descend to the earth, containing the strength of the high and the low, he means by this the breathing in (istinshaq) of the air, and the taking of the spirit from it, and its subsequent elevation to the highest degree of heat, and it is the Fire, and the low is the body, and its content of the controlling earthly power which imparts the colours. For there lie in it those higher powers, as well as the earthly powers which were submerged in it.

The natural operation and decay causes it to be manifest, and hence the strength of the earth, and of the air, and of the higher fire passed in to it. Later he said [#9] it will overcome the high and the low because in it is found the light of lights: and consequently the darkness will flee from it.

[See Stapleton et al. 1949, p 74, 81.]

APPENDIX

Translation from Roger Bacon's edition of *Secretum Secretorum* made c. 1445

1)Trouth hath hym so, and it is no doubt,

2) that the lower is to the heigher, and the heigher to the lower aunsweren.

The worcher forsoth of all myracles is the one and sool God, of and fro Whom Cometh all meruelous operacions.

3) So all thynges were created of o soole substance, and of o soole disposicion,

4) the fader wherof is the sone, and the moone moder,

5) that brought hym forth by blast or aier in the wombe, the erthe taken fro it,

6) to whom is seid the increat fader, tresour of myracles, and yever of vertues.

7) Of fire is made erthe.

7a) Depart the erthe fro the fire, for the sotiller is worthier than the more grosse, and the thynne thynge than the thik. This most be do wisely and discretly.

8) It ascendith fro the erth into the heven, and falleth fro heven to the erthe, and therof sleith the higher and the lower vertue.

9)And yf it lordship in the lower and in the heigher, and thow shalt lordship aboue and beneth, which forsoth is the light of lightes, and therfor fro the wolle fle all derknesse.

10) The higher vertue ouer-cometh all, for sothe all thynne thyng doth in dense thynges.

11a) After the disposicion of the more world rynneth this worchyng.

13) And for this prophetisyng of the trynyte of God Hermogenes it called Triplex, trebil in philosophie, as Aristotle seith.

[See Manzalaoui 1977: 65 -6.]

Translation of same source, made c. 1485.

1) The trwthe is so, and that it is no dowght,

2) that lower thyngis to hyer thyng, and hyer to lower be correspondent. But the Werker of myraclis is on Godde alone, fro Home descendyth euiry meruulus werk.

3)And so alle thyngis be creat of one only substauns, be an only dysposicion,

4) of home the fadyr is the sonne, and the mone the modyr,

5) qwyche bar her be the wedyr in the wombe. The erthe is priuyd fro her-to.

6)This is clepyd or seyd the fadyr of enchauntmentis, tresur of myracclys, the yessuer of vertuys.

7) Be a lytil it is made erthe.

7a) Depart that qwyche is erthly fro that qwyche is firy, for that qwyche is

111

sotel is mor wurthy han that qwyche is grose, and that rar, porous, or lyght, is mor bettyr than qwiche is thyk of substauns. This is done wyseli or dyscretly.

8) It ascendyth fro the erth in-to heuyn and fallyth fro heuyn in-to erth, and ther-of it sleth the ouyr vertu and the nedyr vertu, so it hath lorchyp in the lowe thyngis and hye thingis,

9) and thu lordschyppist vppeward and downward, and with the is the lyght of lyghtys. And for that alle derkness schal fle fro the.

10) The ovyr vetu ouircomyth alle, for euiry rar thyng werkyth in to euiry thyk thyng.

11a) And aftyr the dysposicion of the mor world rennyth thys werking.

13) And for that Hermogines is clepyd threfold in filosophye, and of the meruellys of he world.

[See Manzalaoui 1977: 174-5]

BIBLIOGRAPHY

Albertus Magnus, *Book of Minerals*, trans D. Wyckoff, OUP, 1967.

Anon. *Meditations on the Tarot*. Amity House, 1985 pp21-6

Brann, N.L. "George Ripley and the Abbot Trithemius", *Ambix*, vol 26, no 3, pp 212- 220, 1979.

Blavatsky, H.P. *Isis Unveiled*. Theosophical University Press, 1972.

Burckhardt, T. *Alchemy*. Stuart and Watkins, London 1967 pp 196 -201.

Davis, Tenny L. "The Emerald Tablet of Hermes Tristmegistus: Three Latin versions which were current among later Alchemists", *Journal of Chemical Education,* Vol.3, no.8, pp 863-75, 1926.

de Jong, H.M.E. *Michael Maiers's Atlanta Fugiens: Sources of an alchemical Book of Emblems*. E.J. Brill, Leiden, 1969.

Dobbs, B.J. "Newton's Commentary on the Emerald Tablet of Hermes Trismegistus" in Merkel, I and Debus A.G. *Hermeticism and the Renaissance.* Folger, Washington 1988.

Fulcanelli. *Les Demeures Philosophales*. Jean Jacques Pavert, Paris, 1964.

Hall, M.P. *The Secret Teachings of all Ages*. Philosophical Research, L.A. 1977 pp CLVII -CLVIII.

Holmyard, E.J. "The Emerald Table" *Nature*, Oct 6th pp 525-6, 1929.

Holmyard, E.J. *Alchemy*, Pelican, Harmondsworth 1957. pp95-8.

Linden, Stanton J. ed. *The Mirror of Alchimy Composed by the Thrice-Famous and Learned Fryer Roger Bacon* (1597), Garland, NY. 1992.

Manzalaoui, M.A. *Secretum Secretorum: Nine English Versions*, Early English Text Society. OUP, 1977.

Needham, J. *Science and Civilisation in China.* vol 5, part 4: Spagyrical discovery and invention: Apparatus, Theories and gifts. CUP, 1980

Read, John *Prelude to Chemistry*, G Bell, London, 1939, pp15, 51-5

Redgrove, S. *Alchemy: Ancient and Modern.* William Rider, London, 1922, pp40-42.

Sadoul, J. *Alchemists and Gold.* G.P. Putnams, N.Y. 1972, pp 25-6.

Schumaker, Wayne. *The Occult Sciences in the Renaissance.* University of California, Berkely 1972, pp 179-80

Shah, Idres. *The Sufis.* Octagon, London 1977, p 198

Sherwood Taylor, F. *The Alchemists.* Paladin, London, 1976, pp77- 8.

Stapleton, H.E., Lewis, G.L, Sherwood Taylor, F. "The sayings of Hermes quoted in the Ma Al-Waraqi of Ibn Umail. " *Ambix*, vol 3, pp 69-90, 1949.

Steele, R. and Singer, D.W. "The Emerald Table". *Proceedings of the Royal Society of Medicine* vol 21, 1928.

See also:

McLean, A & Tahil, P. *Ampitheatre Engavings of Heinrich Kunrath.* pp. 28, 73-6

Anon, *Secret Symbols of the Rosicrucians* (i.e., Paul Allen *A Christian Rosenkreutz Anthology,* Steinerbooks, third edition pp228-30)

AMORC Supplementary Monograph: *Hermetic Teachings* RAD-13, Lecture Number 2, Inner hermetic teachings.

AZILOTH ||||| BOOKS

Aziloth Books publishes a wide range of titles ranging from hard-to-find esoteric books - Parchment Books - to classic works on fiction, politics and philosophy - Cathedral Classics. Our newest venture is Aziloth Books Children's Classics, with vibrant new covers and Black-and-White/Colour illustrations to complement some of the world's very best children's tales. All our imprints are offered to the reader at a competitive price and through as many mediums and outlets as possible.

We are committed to excellent book production and strive, whenever possible, to add value to our titles with original images, maps and author introductions. With the premium on space in most modern dwellings, we also endeavour - within the limits of good book design - to make our products as slender as possible, allowing more books to be fitted into a given bookshelf area.

We are a small, approachable company and would love to hear any of your comments and suggestions on our plans, products, or indeed on absolutely anything. We look forward to meeting you.

Contact us at: info@azilothbooks.com.

PARCHMENT BOOKS enshrines the concept of the oneness of all true religious traditions - that "the light shines from many different lanterns". Our list below offers titles from both eastern and western spiritual traditions, including Christian, Judaic, Islamic, Daoist, Hindu and Buddhist mystical texts, as well as books on alchemy, hermeticism, paganism, etc..

By bringing together such spiritual texts, we hope to make esoteric and occult knowledge more readily available to those ready to receive it. We do not publish grimoires or any titles pertaining to the left hand path. Titles include:

Abandonment to Divine Providence	Jean-Pierre de Caussade
Corpus Hermeticum	G.R.S. Mead (trans.)
The Holy Rule of St Benedict	St. Benedict of Nursia
Kundalini	G. S. Arundale
The Way of Perfection	St. Teresa of Avila
Q.B.L.	Frater Achad
The Cloud Upon the Sanctuary	Karl von Eckhartshausen
The Confession of St Patrick	St. Patrick
Nightmare Tales; The Voice of the Silence	H. P. Blavatsky
The Outline of Sanity	G K Chesterton
The Teachings of Zoroaster	Shapuji A Kapadia
The Dialogue Of St Catherine Of Siena	St. Catherine of Siena
Esoteric Christianity	Annie Besant
The Wisdom of the Egyptians	Brian Brown
The Spiritual Exercises of St. Ignatius	St. Ignatius of Loyola
Dark Night of the Soul	St. John of the Cross
Moses and Monotheism	Sigmund Freud
Man, His True Nature & Ministry	Louis-Claude de St.-Martin
The Gospel of Thomas	Anonymous
Alchemy Rediscovered and Restored	Archibald Cockren
The Imitation of Christ	Thomas à Kempis
The Interior Castle	St. Teresa of Avila
Songs of Innocence & Experience	William Blake
De Rerum Natura	Lucretius
The Secret of the Rosary	St. Louis de Montfort
Tertium Organum	P. D. Ouspensky
From Ritual to Romance	Jessie L. Weston
The God of the Witches	Margaret Murray
De Anima (Concerning the Soul)	Aristotle

Obtainable at all good online and local bookstores.
View Aziloth Books' full list at: www.azilothbooks.com

CATHEDRAL CLASSICS hosts an array of classic literature, from erudite ancient tomes to avant-garde, twentieth-century masterpieces, all of which deserve a place in your home. All the world's great novelists are here, Jane Austen, Dickens, Conrad, Arthur Machen and Henry James, brushing shoulders with such disparate luminaries as Sun Tzu, Marcus Aurelius, Kipling, Friedrich Nietzsche, Machiavelli, and Omar Khayam. A small selection is detailed below:

The Prophet	Kahlil Gibran
Herland	Charlotte Perkins Gilman
With Her in Ourland	Charlotte Perkins Gilman
Frankenstein	Mary Shelley
The Time Machine; The Invisible Man	H. G. Wells
Three Men in a Boat	Jerome K Jerome
The Rubaiyat of Omar Khayyam	Omar Khayyam
A Study in Scarlet	Arthur Conan Doyle
Persuasion	Jane Austen
The Picture of Dorian Gray	Oscar Wilde
Flatland	Edwin A. Abbott
The Coming Race	Bulwer Lytton
The Adventures of Sherlock Holmes	Arthur Conan Doyle
The Great God Pan	Arthur Machen
Beyond Good and Evil	Friedrich Nietzsche
England, My England	D. H. Lawrence
The Castle of Otranto	Horace Walpole
Self-Reliance, & Other Essays (series1&2)	Ralph W. Emmerson
The Art of War	Sun Tzu
A Shepherd's Life	W. H. Hudson
The Double	Fyodor Dostoyevsky
To the Lighthouse; Mrs Dalloway	Virginia Woolf
The Sorrows of Young Werther	Johann W. Goethe
Leaves of Grass - 1855 edition	Walt Whitman
Analects	Confucius
Beowulf	Anonymous
Agnes Grey	Anne Bronte
Plain Tales From The Hills	Rudyard Kipling
The Subjection of Women	John Stuart Mill
Silas Marner	George Eliot
The Rights of Man	Thomas Paine
Herland	Charlotte Perkins Gilman

Obtainable at all good online and local bookstores.
View Aziloth Books' full list at: www.azilothbooks.com

AZILOTH CHILDREN'S CLASSICS Aziloth Books is passionate about bringing the very best in children's classics fiction to the next generation of book-lovers. Renowned for its original design and outstanding quality, our highly successful list has something to suit every age and interest. Titles include:

The Railway Children	Edith Nesbit
5 Children and It	Edith Nesbit
Anne of Green Gables	Lucy Maud Montgomery
What Katy Did	Susan Coolidge
What Katy Did Next	Susan Coolidge
Puck of Pook's Hill	Rudyard Kipling
The Jungle Books	Rudyard Kipling
Just So Stories	Rudyard Kipling
Alice Through the Looking Glass	Charles Dodgson
Alice's Adventures in Wonderland	Charles Dodgson
Black Beauty	Anna Sewell
The War of the Worlds	H. G Wells
The Time Machine	H. G .Wells
The Sleeper Awakes	H. G. Wells
The Invisible Man	H. G. Wells
The Lost World	Sir Arthur Conan Doyle
A Christmas Carol	Charles Dickens
Call of the Wild	Jack London
Greenmantle	John Buchan
Treasure Island	Robert Louis Stevenson
Dr Jekyll and Mr Hyde	Robert Louis Stevenson
Gulliver's Travels	Jonathan Swift
Catriona (David Balfour)	Robert Louis Stevenson
The Water Babies	Charles Kingsley
The First Men in the Moon	Jules Verne
The Secret Garden	Frances Hodgson Burnett
A Little Princess	Frances Hodgson Burnett
Peter Pan	J. M. Barrie

Obtainable at all good online and local bookstores.
View Aziloth Books' full list at: www.azilothbooks.com

www.ingramcontent.com/pod-product-compliance
Lightning Source LLC
Chambersburg PA
CBHW060115050426
42448CB00010B/1877